W0007971

CASE METHOD^{SM} FAST-TRACK

A RAD Approach

About the Authors

Dai Clegg was born in Preston, England, in 1953. He received a B.Sc. in Mathematics from Birmingham University and later an M.Sc. in Computer Science from the University of London. Dai has worked in the software industry for twenty years and has gained wide experience in a variety of companies in the public and private sector, in user organizations and in service companies. In 1988 he joined Oracle's CASE product development group with responsibility for product definition. He still has that responsibility but retains real-world contact at seminars and conferences around the world and by involvement with Oracle customers.

Richard Barker was born in Sheffield, England, in 1946. He went to Edinburgh University where he studied Chemistry, but realized that his interests lay outside the realms of pure science.

He has gained insight into many aspects of information systems through work in manufacturing industry and the Health Service, and the early introduction of database and data dictionary software whilst working with a major hardware company. Subsequently, Richard led a consultancy team specializing in strategic analysis and systems development using structured methods. He is an acknowledged expert in database and CASE technology and their practical application. He was a founder director of Oracle UK and led the development of the CASE Method and CASE tools for ten years. Richard established the UK Training Division to provide education for clients and Oracle staff alike in the use of Oracle products, methods and strategic thinking, and has lectured widely on network and relational database technology, distributed databases, CASE and user involvement in systems development. He is now in the position of Senior Vice-President at OpenVision where he has turned his attention to managing complex systems, which might have been built using CASE and database technology and must operate reliably and securely on a global scale.

Barbara Barker was born in Coleraine, Northern Ireland, in 1946. She studied Biochemistry at Edinburgh University. She has worked in a laboratory, been a teacher, a technical editor and an environmental activist, with a continuing involvement in wildlife conservation work. Richard and Barbara are married with three children, and live in Berkshire, England. They have worked together for several years on this series of books.

CASE METHOD^{SM}
FAST-TRACK

A RAD Approach

DAI CLEGG
RICHARD BARKER

 Addison-Wesley Publishing Company

Wokingham, England • Reading, Massachusetts • Menlo Park, California
New York • Don Mills, Ontario • Amsterdam • Bonn • Sydney • Singapore
Tokyo • Madrid • San Juan • Milan • Paris • Mexico City • Seoul • Taipei

ORACLE®

The Relational Database Management System

Many of the designations used by manufacturers and sellers to distinguish their products are claimed as trademarks. Addison-Wesley has made every attempt to supply trademark information about manufacturers and their products mentioned in this book. A list of the trademark designations and their owners appears on p. xiv.

Cover designed by Hybert Design & Type, Maidenhead and printed by The Riverside Printing Co. (Reading) Ltd.
Printed in The United States of America.

First printed 1994.

Written by Dai Clegg, Richard Barker and Barbara Barker. Edited and illustrated by Barbara Barker.

ISBN 0-201-62432-X

Britsh Library Cataloguing in Publication Data
A catalogue record for this book is available from the British Library.

Library of Congress Cataloguing in Publication Data applied for.

Other books available in the CASE Method series:
  Tasks and Deliverables
  Entity Relationship Modelling
  Function and Process Modelling

When ordering this book through Oracle Corporation please quote the Part Number A20925

Contact:

Oracle Corporation UK Ltd
The Oracle Centre
The Ring
Bracknell
Berkshire RG12 1BW
UK

World Headquarters
Oracle Corporation
500 Oracle Parkway
Redwood Shores, CA 94065
USA

FOREWORD

In every computer department around the world management is demanding new and better systems yesterday! Many of these systems are parts of integrated, mission-critical, operational environments and need to be approached with much care and rigour. But in today's rapidly changing business world there is a trend towards loosely coupled small systems which are built quickly and changed frequently to react to urgent user demands. It is on this area that Information Systems management must concentrate to maintain their own credibility within their companies and to demonstrate that they are, for once, an **asset** to their organizations rather than a liability – otherwise known as a **cost centre**.

The reasons for the business pressure are wide and varied. Perhaps the major root cause of the changes we see is that global communication is now virtually instantaneous and very cheap. In my home and office, for example, I have seven telephone systems catering for modems, facsimile machines, automatic security systems and for carrying with me on trips. From my car in England I can talk to a colleague flying in a Boeing 747 somewhere over Texas, and yet it is not so long ago that only one home in five would have a telephone and perhaps twenty employees in an office would share the same device. The telephone is not the sole culprit. Global market news is available to anyone via television or, for more precise information, from the various international financial agencies that sell the required services across the 'wire'. Fast moving multinationals use twenty-four-hour worldwide electronic mail, multiple-point video conferencing and sophisticated distributed computerized database systems to give them a competitive edge. In my current software development unit we have people working in concert even though some are based in England and some in the United States of America. For design reviews, brainstorming or serious planning, however, there is still no substitute for face-to-face interaction – but that is no great problem with modern travel and so the aeroplane and the motor car must also share in the blame. If I have a new system design I want to discuss with a colleague back at base whilst I am travelling, it would be neat to get in touch from the aeroplane flying over the Atlantic and connect my laptop into the development database back at base so we can both work on the design schematic on our own screens. Maybe next year.

These impressive advances in communications are reflected in changes of attitude in companies, governments and across international boundaries. The signing of NAFTA, the removal of obstacles towards GATT and the emergence of the newly industrialized Asian Pacific nations are among the events contributing to huge changes in the global economic environment; changes that are bringing unprecedented pressures to bear on companies to stay competitive.

So what can business do? It is really very simple. Companies must reduce unit costs, improve quality, innovate and concentrate on their core competencies, yet rapidly exploit new niche opportunities as they arise. They must grasp relevant new technologies and apply them faster than their competitors. They must react to the consumer demand for higher quality and customer-oriented timely service – today the customer is king, not the product. And they must address their infrastructures and, without regard to their current practice, redesign their key business processes to produce dramatic improvements in business indicators such as 'time to market', 'customer satisfaction', 'market share' and 'profit per employee'.

Business issues such as these are causing a revolution in the way people use computer systems. The goal is often the deployment to the business of relevant user-oriented systems in a timely manner, exploiting the currently accepted ideal combination of relational database, client/server and graphical user interfaces. And where those systems must be tightly or loosely coupled, to have the confidence that after phase I is implemented there will not be a major upheaval during the introduction of phases II and III. This calls for an approach and a set of complementary tools that combine powerful yet simple business modelling capability, concentration on the essence of the problem, close cooperation between executive, user and developer, rapid and iterative prototyping. This approach will also exploit code generators, using computer-driven style guides and preferences for other good practice to produce high–quality systems from small self-directed teams.

Over the years many attempts have been made to meet these goals, with varying levels of success. Today, for the first time, there is sufficient power in our desktop and server technology to enable the meta information that we provide to the system building tools to be used to create sophisticated, performant, function rich and usable applications that are aesthetically pleasing to use. The key to success is the ability to hold cross-related information about the need in a shared repository and to automatically exploit each fact in as many ways as is sensible.

Let's look at a detailed example. The definition of an order line on an order will normally include a relationship to either a known type of product or service. This fact can therefore be used in many circumstances, and if business circumstances change we can alter the detail about the fact in the repository and all the affected code can be brought into line automatically, to represent the new business rule faithfully. This obviously has a dramatic impact on the productivity and completeness of new systems, and on the ease and accuracy of maintenance. The generator technology can also infer much more from a single fact. For a product in our example, we will already have defined its data attributes, validation rules, normal screen display characteristics and whether, for example, each product might have some multimedia information such as an image or a video clip held about it.

So for our simple order-line-to-product relationship a good CASE tool (or with an older approach, a good designer/programmer) could automatically do the following. Wherever an order line appears on a screen the tool would create, say, a fixed length field for the six-character product code and a second sideways scrolling field with display length sixteen characters and a maximum capacity of forty characters for the relevant product description. Wherever a product code is entered, the tool would insert rules to validate that it is an existing code, giving a meaningful in-context error message when the code is not valid. On the screen, the tool would place a 'button' and/or allow a function key to provide a valid list of product code values on request to save typing and mistakes. On that 'list of values' popup window it could show the user the description and the recommended price and allow the list to be subset quickly by partial search criteria on the description and price (e.g. %video% and <$500). The screen could also implicitly provide a fastpath route to the full details of the product, including a photographic image and full technical text of the one the user is interested in. The layout of each of the screens referencing an order line will have automatically put the order-line details in the same sequence, with the same prompt and help text, in the same colour and font, and within a suitably laid out frame so that it is obvious what data is related. If required by the company's standards, the tool can also have arranged that the user can create the details of a new product previously unknown to the system whilst still in the order-line context, typically following the message about a non-existent product. Behind the scenes, on the database, any update of product usage may be causing server-side code to check stock balances, and if insufficient to send out instructions to manufacture more.

The tools need facts about the business and a rule base of good practice to enable them to generate the implied code, layout and user interface, and to be able to execute the millions of lines of code needed to accomplish this difficult design task quickly to give the desired result.

The approach covered in this book is based on the experience of practitioners familiar with these rich business modelling concepts, communicating effectively with users and exploiting to the full the combination of relational database technology, CASE tools and modern graphical user interfaces. The technologies, however, are less important than the concept of creating rapid deployment teams that take a business problem and then model it; synthesize a solution, and prototype, check and incrementally generate a system against difficult business deadlines.

But apply with caution. This approach works well where the scope is contained and there are clearly defined interfaces to other systems with which it must be loosely coupled. It requires small teams of practitioners of better than average expertise, each of whom is capable of covering many aspects of the work, and close cooperation with the right users – the ones that really know what is needed and can, with the team, make quick decisions on timeliness, functionality, usability, performance and other trade-offs. The aim is to build an adequate usable system quickly – not a perfect system too late for the business.

Increased rigour must be used if complex multi-system integration is necessary. More checks and balances must be applied if inexperienced teams are used. Non-standard design refinements may be necessary if the system is to be implemented across multiple sites. And different tools may be needed if the target is not to be implemented in the way envisaged by this particular tool; for example, the Oracle CASE tool is not currently designed to generate shopfloor process control systems.

The way forward is to focus on a combination of developers, users and executives who really understand what the business needs and what modern technology can do to help. They can then decide which projects are suited to this style of fast-track approach and which projects are better served by a more formal approach. The decision, in the end, must always be a business one. What is the risk to the business of not having an operational system by a given date, versus the risk of trusting a small team working to produce it quickly?

Richard Barker
July 1994

PREFACE

In writing this book I tried to achieve two different objectives. The first objective was to provide an overview of fast-track, the techniques it applies, and particularly the management challenges it presents. The second objective was to provide a handbook for project managers running fast-track projects. Putting these together might have endangered the second, and more pragmatic objective. This I did not want to do, so the book is split into two distinct parts. Chapters 1 to 3 deal with fast-track in general, Chapters 4 to 7 deal with the life-cycle of a project in more detail, identifying the tasks and their deliverables, the techniques and the tools that support them. These later chapters refer back to the relevant sections of the first part of the book so the descriptions of specific techniques are all gathered together in Chapter 3 and not scattered and duplicated through subsequent chapters.

I hope that this structure will mean a casual reader can gain an understanding of the fast-track approach quickly from the first part of the book, and the practitioner can have an organized and compact reference for daily use from the second part.

In assembling the second part I frequently found myself adding an extra step or an additional task, for completeness. The result is that, while not all projects will need every step of every task, they are all necessary under some circumstances. Every task is included in a project on the basis of what it produces. If a particular project has no need of the result, for example, documentation of test results, then it should not be produced and the task should be omitted. During the initial planning of a project the template project plan offered in Chapters 4 to 6 should be assessed and tailored for the project, cutting out the unnecessary tasks and steps. Do not be afraid to prune. The questions to ask are: *"Do I need this deliverable to manage the project?"* and *"Does the sponsor value this deliverable above its price?"*

I have used Oracle tools throughout in examples, and in particular I have recommended an approach that exploits the ability of the Oracle CASE tools to define rules once and then reuse them many times. Some CASE tools do not exploit reusability in this way, but the trend in development technology is towards greater reusability so it seems very appropriate here.

Dai Clegg
July 1994

CONTENTS

Foreword . . . . **v**

Preface . . . . **ix**

Chapter 1   **Introduction** **1**

What Is a Method? 1

Why Use a Method? 2

What Is a Fast-track Method? 2

How Does Fast-track Relate to CASE Method? 5

What Are the Characteristics of Fast-track? 7

What Makes a Fast-track Project? 12

Fast-track and CASE Tools 14

Chapter 2   **Management of Fast-track Projects** . . . . **.15**

The Project Development Life-cycle 15

Scoping the Project 19

Partitioning the Project 21

Estimating in Fast-track Projects 24

Controlling Formal, Iterative and Timebox Builds 25

Quality Management in Fast-track Projects 27

Summary 30

Chapter 3 **Fast-track Techniques** **31**

General Professional Skills 32

CASE Method Techniques 38

Specific Fast-track Techniques 49

Summary 71

Chapter 4 **Planning Stage** **73**

Overview 73

Objectives 74

Major Deliverables 74

Critical Success Factors 76

The Tasks 76

Summary 94

Chapter 5 **Requirements Stage** **95**

Overview 95

Objectives 96

Major Deliverables 96

Critical Success Factors 99

The Sub-stages and Tasks 99

Summary 126

Chapter 6 **Build Stage** **127**

Overview 127

Objectives 127

Major Deliverables 127

Critical Success Factors 129

The Sub-stages and Tasks 129

Summary 164

Chapter 7 **Completing the Life-cycle** **165**

Transition 165

Hyper Fast-track 168

One-shot Fast-track 170

Chapter 8   **The Next Step** **173**

Implementing Fast-track 173

Making the Change 175

In Conclusion 179

Appendix A   **Timesaving Hints & Tips** **181**

Appendix B   **Using Other Books in the CASE Method Series** **185**

Bibliography **189**

Glossary of Terms **191**

Index **203**

1 Introduction

Information systems have become essential to the operation of all kinds of enterprises. In business and in government, in factories and in offices computer-based information systems provide speedy and reliable execution of a whole host of tasks. An organization without computerization would be unable to compete effectively on cost or to provide the best value for money to its customers. Many of these systems evolved over a long period of time to meet the needs of relatively stable businesses and are now operating satisfactorily, even though the initial cost of development was high.

Developing information systems to meet the **real** needs of organizations is a relatively young discipline. It has come a long way in a short time but still has a long way to go before any given complex computer systems development project can be assured of success. This is one goal of information system developers: can we get to the position where computer systems are engineered, rather than crafted? To reach that goal we need a teachable and repeatable definition of what needs to be done in order to complete a successful computer systems development project. Such a definition is known as a Methodology or Method.

What Is a Method?

A method is a set of rules, instructions, examples and any other information necessary to enable a less experienced practitioner to benefit from the experience of others. It is a formalization of the best practice available at the time. Of course, the technology available to the systems engineering profession is constantly changing. Early methodologies were based on implementations for file systems, but as database technology matured and particularly relational database technology, the techniques and processes of systems engineering have changed too; for example, entity relationship modelling is now a widely used standard for data modelling.

Early methods were entirely paper based. Then came the application of computer technology to support and automate systems engineering itself – Computer-Aided Systems Engineering (CASE). So best practice changed to exploit the automation that CASE brings, which means that methods cannot exist independently of the technologies that they are applied to, or of the technologies that they use. Methods themselves must be developed and updated in order to represent current best practice in the profession.

CASE Method is an example of a method that has successfully helped to formalize information systems development.

Why Use a Method?

A structured information systems development method helps because it provides a staged approach, with identifiable deliverables to be produced at each stage, with specified tasks to be carried out in order to create those deliverables, and with additional techniques for measuring the success of the process and the quality of the deliverables. A good method assists the project manager in identifying the required deliverables and in estimating the time and resources necessary to produce them. This provides the means for managing the process and reducing the risks. A well-structured method also provides an approach that matches the way a flexible organization runs: it is driven by the key people at all levels of the organization who know what needs to be done, and cross-checked against existing working practices and systems.

The first successful methods, such as CASE Method, Information Engineering (IE) and the Structured Systems Analysis and Design Methodology (SSADM) share a life-cycle model of stages, or phases, following one after the other. This life-cycle model has become known as the waterfall life-cycle model, because of the implication of information flowing downwards from one stage to the next, as illustrated in Figure 1-1 opposite.

What Is a Fast-track Method?

Just as we feel confident that we can rise to the challenge of successful development of useful information systems, we are overtaken by history. Because business, technology and the expectations and needs of computer systems users are changing at an ever increasing rate, systems development must be increasingly rapid and flexible.

One of the original goals of structured methods was to reduce the considerable risks associated with building information systems, by making the process predictable, repeatable and learnable. In short, they tried to introduce engineering principles to what had been a black art, and they have succeeded to a greater or lesser extent. In so doing they have improved productivity across the full systems life-cycle, from inception to production, by reducing the errors introduced, and so they have reduced the time and effort involved in testing and debugging.

Figure 1-1
The Waterfall Life-cycle

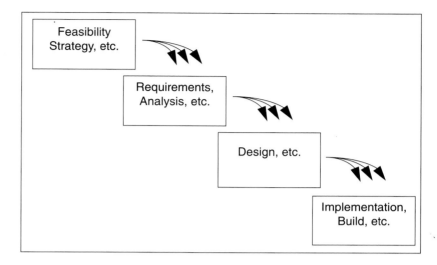

As the systems development methods have matured and their use has become more widespread, the technology for automating the development process has matured. Initially, CASE tools were developed to automate the processes as defined in systems development methods. But the technology quickly reached a stage where it was possible to challenge the existing methods and to make new approaches possible. CASE tools now offer the prospect of re-engineering the business of information systems development. They offer the opportunity to make the transition to the next stage in the process of formalizing information systems development. The fast-track approach places the emphasis firmly on exploiting CASE for productivity, without sacrificing the risk reduction achieved with structured methods.

During the 1980s there was a great deal of interest from a wide variety of sources in improving the waterfall life-cycle model. There was the beginning of the serious promotion of prototyping in the life-cycle, for example Budde et al (1991). There were alternative life-cycles to the waterfall, such as the spiral life-cycle, where iterations of the system gradually arrive at the required solution, proposed by Boehm (1988). In the commercial world the development of existing methods to develop and exploit these new ideas resulted in Rapid Application Development (RAD) as an addition to Information Engineering (IE) (Martin, 1991), Rapid Systems Development (RSD) (Gane, 1987) and CASE Method Fast-track.

Early methods reduced the risks of information systems development so that technology could be harnessed to real business objectives. Fast-track provides the quantum jump in productivity which is necessary to respond to a rate of change that borders on chaos.

Figure 1-2 illustrates how the original structured methods and the later addition of fast-track approaches have improved risk management and productivity in information systems development.

Figure 1-2
Risk and Productivity

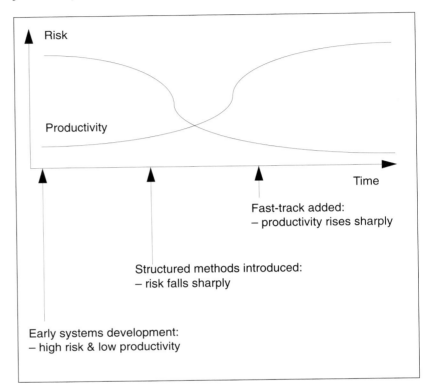

Example:

Hotel Guest Administration

A major international hotel chain has recently acquired a number of smaller chains, and has identified the need for an integrated Guest Administration System. A team of analysts has been set the task of defining the requirements and scope for the new system. They have a high–level function decomposition as guidance, but in investigating the various different ways that the hotels in the group operate currently it becomes clear that different approaches are being used. The analysts feel that their best option is to clarify the requirement before defining the development project in detail. Using the code generation capability of the CASE tool they used to record their initial analysis of the requirement, they create a prototype Guest Registration System. They do not spend time on user interface design, but let the generator default it from the guidelines for user interface design which have been recorded in the CASE tool for previous projects. The generated prototype manages all the information specified in the analysis and provides facilities to support the different tasks that reception desk staff need to perform: validate payment method, record guest preferences, allocate appropriate accommodation.

Our analysts set up the prototype at the company's staff training centre, and during quiet moments in the training courses take the opportunity to show the prototype to staff from many different hotels in the chain and from many different levels of experience and seniority. In a very short period of time they get comments and insights from a wide and representative cross-section of the eventual user community. Using the CASE tools and its generators, they incorporate the changes suggested and evolve the prototype day by day, almost hour by hour.

This use of prototyping is known as requirements prototyping. We are using the prototype to provoke reaction, to confirm or correct, and to complete our understanding of the need. This is the fast-track approach in action, finding a swifter way to assure ourselves that the analysts' understanding of Guest Registration really meets the needs of the people who do that job and their management. The existence of generator technology that could be driven from high-level definitions of the business requirement meant that rapid evolutionary prototyping was not only possible, but resulted in a stable and consistent documentation set that could be reused in the eventual implementation, even if the prototype itself was discarded.

In this example we did not discuss how the initial understanding was reached. The analysts could have conducted group interviews in the form of workshops with representative users, perhaps lasting a day at a time. In the workshops the requirements would be identified, discussed and prioritized. This would illustrate another aspect of fast-track in action, which was not dependent on new CASE technology so much as on a better understanding of group dynamics and the interpersonal skills needed to conduct workshop sessions successfully. In the Guest Registration example this was not the approach taken; the analysts conducted some representative interviews with opinion leaders in the user community and quickly gained enough information to build the prototype. It would have been more expensive and ultimately slower to get sufficient representative users and managers together for these intensive workshops than for the analysts to travel to the users. Fast-track is not about slavish use of new techniques for the sake of novelty. It must be an appropriate technique and its use must not raise the level of risk unnecessarily.

How Does Fast-track Relate to CASE Method?

The short history of the information technology industry is littered with examples of 'new lamps for old', of new technology being presented as a panacea and the replaced technology as having been flawed from concept. The fast-track approach should not fall into this trap. It builds on the successes of CASE Method in defining the life-cycle and developing a deliverables-oriented approach. The same basic life-cycle remains as do many of the tasks. However, fast-track modifies the life-cycle to exploit alternative techniques that have been proven in practice and particularly techniques that use evolutionary iterations, often known as 'iterative build', to produce deliverables.

Iterative Build

The iterative build approach mirrors more closely what happens in the rapidly changing real world. In practice, most project requirements definitions are challenged during design and most designs are challenged and changed, often before they even get off the drawing board. CASE tools and structured development methods have given us ways of controlling and managing such change.

Fast-track goes further; it embraces change. We should accept that change is inevitable and should, therefore, mould our working practices to respond positively to change, not to resist it. In the example above, because the prototype was easy to construct and easy to change, our team of analysts could encourage users to review and criticize it, the result being that the system that they will eventually develop will be closer to what is really needed, will need less modification and, critically, will meet with a high degree of user acceptance early on.

Timeboxing

A complementary strategy to iterative development, which can be folded into fast-track projects, is the use of timeboxing. A timebox development is one in which a skilled and motivated team is assembled and targets a particular goal by a particular date.

All projects have 3 interdependent variables:

- the Deliverables – what the project must produce
- the Resources – what people, materials and money are available
- the Timescale – when the deliverables must be produced by

We can shorten the timescale by increasing the resources or cutting down the deliverables. We can increase the deliverables by extending the time and adding resources. Time, unfortunately, is not elastic. The scope of a project, defined in terms of its deliverables, often appears to be elastic, but if we seem to be getting more for less, then quality is being sacrificed. We can move the three variables, but always, what we gain in one dimension we lose in another. Timeboxing fixes the resources and the timescale and prioritizes the deliverables. By this strategy the project deliverables are a function of the productivity of the resources. Hence these should be the very best available, in terms of working environment, tools and human expertise, and the people themselves must be highly motivated to succeed. It should be noted that simple monetary reward is not always the best way to supply that motivation. More complex rewards may be necessary, including such aspects as prestige, career opportunities, and rest and recreation time. Timeboxing is a valid way of tackling discrete, bounded projects or sub-projects by applying high-quality resources to a complex problem over a fixed time.

Risk Adaptive Management

Another major difference in fast-track is the project management approach. As we noted earlier, the primary objective of the original development methods was risk reduction, and elimination where possible. Fast-track differs in that it adopts a more flexible strategy which is best described as risk adaptive as opposed to risk aversive. There is intrinsically more risk in the evolutionary approach. It is impossible to know for certain in advance how many iterations will be necessary, but, provided the number of iterations is low, the exploitation of faster techniques means a net gain. However, modern project management techniques focus on deliverables and it is difficult to assess partial deliverables, in the form of intermediate prototypes. The old adage of project management that every task is eighty percent complete for eighty percent of the time springs to mind. Timeboxing is one useful response to this problem, but fast-track also introduces other ways of measuring progress during iterative development which can provide managers with key indicators of the performance of a project without inventing artificial, intermediate deliverables that will slow the team down.

Life-cycle User Involvement

The third departure is in user involvement. The profile of user involvement in well-run development projects has tended to be high in the early requirements stages, dropping fairly dramatically during design and build, and reviving during testing and implementation. In fast-track projects, the level of user involvement stays high throughout. This is because users are, in effect, participating in acceptance testing from start to finish. Because of the shorter timescales of fast-track projects, the total user involvement will typically be lower; however, the level remains high throughout the project.

What Are the Characteristics of Fast-track?

Risk Adaptive

A fast-track project seeks to balance the complexity of the requirement against speed of implementation, to maximize productivity. Where the scale of the project is very large and the diversity of the user population is great, where the technology is new and the skills unpractised, the risk increases. In such a situation, the fast-track approach identifies ways of managing this risk. For example, in the first phase, we might only satisfy part of the requirement so that the project can be more easily staffed and controlled, or we might only implement for some of the users, so that we can concentrate on a small localized group. In both these cases we deliver benefits early, at low risk, and we are then in a strong position to build on, with lessons learned, with the skills base increased and with a production system to provide feedback and to serve as an example.

Reliant on CASE

CASE tools can do two things for an application developer:

- Firstly, they can automate a task: that is, they can remove the need for a developer to do the task, although there is often still some value that an expert can add to the results. An example of such automation is a Code Generator.

- Secondly, they can support a task that is still carried out by the developer, but enable the developer to do the job better (with fewer errors) or faster, or both. An example of such a tool is a Dataflow Diagrammer.

Most CASE tools have been designed to automate and support techniques and methods already in use, but the development of CASE tool support has started to affect the way that the methods themselves develop. For example, when systems development methodologies were paper based, little use was made of matrix diagrams because they are tedious to create by hand. If, however, a CASE tool can create the matrix automatically, although it cannot derive any insight from the result, it provides a very immediate and visual way to look at the data. Because of this, the methodologies have developed to exploit this aspect of existing CASE tools. Most major CASE tools now include a matrix diagrammer.

Fast-track, being reliant on evolutionary techniques, is much less effective without CASE tool support. For instance, requirements prototypes, such as in the Hotel Guest Registration example above, have often proved to be very costly, both in terms of the effort necessary to create and evolve them and in terms of the unreasonable expectations that they have raised. A good CASE tool that allows developers to create and evolve prototypes quickly, and then retains the definitions of the prototypes as the basis of requirements definition, means that workshops and prototypes become an integral part of requirements definition. The methods evolve to exploit the available CASE technology.

Redefining Systems Development Roles

Conventional applications development practice emphasizes specific roles and skill sets oriented around the stages of the development life-cycle: Strategy, Analysis, Design, and so on. In fast-track, business analysts develop prototypes through to working systems, and technology experts act primarily as systems architects and usability consultants rather than as application designers and coders. Flexibility in the roles of the people is as important as the tools and the techniques. Fast-track increases the challenge to the people involved as much as it increases the opportunities for organizations that exploit it successfully.

Figure 1-3 below illustrates the change in roles between a traditional project and a fast-track project. In fast-track projects, business analysts work with the users throughout the process of requirements definition, through user interface design and development and into user acceptance. They can only do this effectively if their CASE toolkit provides them with the ability to create the early prototypes swiftly from requirements definitions and to refine and evolve these prototypes towards production systems. However, unless the business analyst also possesses all the specialist skills and knowledge of an experienced developer, there may come a time when completion of the development needs these specialist skills: database designers to tune, optimize and perhaps distribute the implemented database; applications design specialists to help define the 'look and feel' style guide and to resolve any application design problems; specialist programmers to complete any custom code, for example, for interfaces to other systems.

Figure 1-3
Redefining Systems
Development Roles

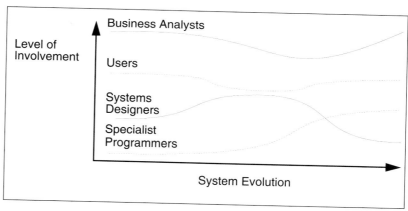

Example:

Integrating a Credit Card Reader

As part of guest registration, the hotel receptionist usually takes a credit card impression. The system requires that this is read in by means of a 'swipe' machine attached to the receptionist's terminal, but with an option for the receptionist to key in the credit card number directly as the guest may have preregistered and provided a credit card number by telephone, the guest may be previously known to the hotel, or the card's magnetic strip may not be readable. Our analysts' prototype will incorporate manual data entry, but it is unlikely that it could have included the swipe reader without specialist programming. However, this requirement can be documented so that it can be developed separately by specialists and integrated later.

The value of the prototype is not diminished, because the front-desk staff can easily explain to the analysts the point at which the swipe machine is needed, and the speed of the development is maintained because the analyst can document the additional requirement and press on.

Figure 1-4
Prototype Guest
Registration Screen

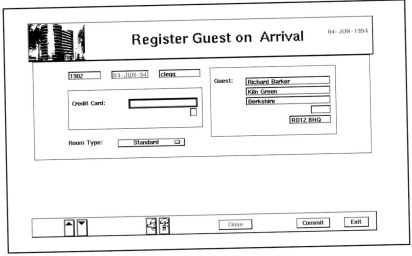

The screen in Figure 1-4 shows the point for entering the credit card number. At this point the prototype does not incorporate the card reader interface so the analyst can make a note of the additional requirement for later inclusion, as in Figure 1-5 below.

Figure 1-5
Record non-Prototyped
Requirement

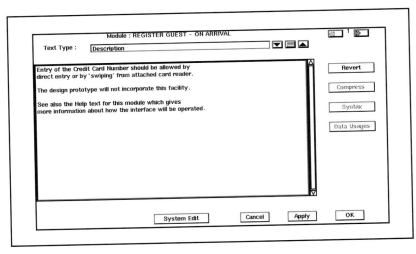

By including the help text (Figure 1-6) at this early stage not only does the analyst save work later, but also gets valuable early feedback; the help is part of the prototype and can be demonstrated for the users and management to ensure that the requirement is properly understood.

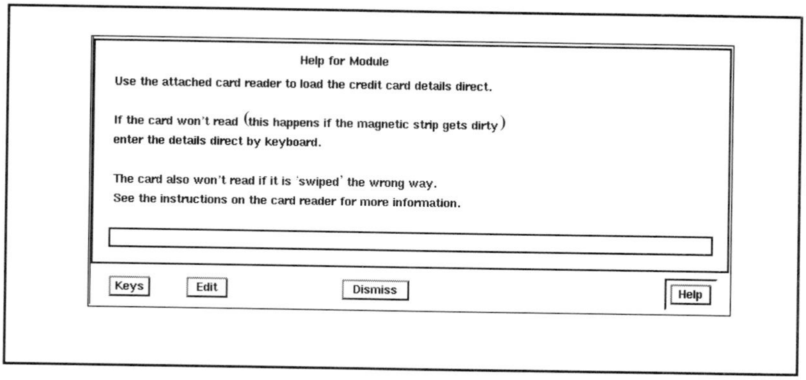

Figure 1-6
Online Help for
Guest Registration

```
                        Help for Module
    Use the attached card reader to load the credit card details direct.

    If the card won't read (this happens if the magnetic strip gets dirty)
    enter the details direct by keyboard.

    The card also won't read if it is 'swiped' the wrong way.
    See the instructions on the card reader for more information.

    [                                                                    ]

    [ Keys ]   [ Edit ]              [ Dismiss ]                 [ Help ]
```

The analyst, equipped with a CASE toolkit, can define the requirements and, using transformer utilities and generators, create systems designs and then production quality code directly from the requirements. We have already identified circumstances where the analyst will rely on specialist programmers to complete particularly complex programming tasks. This scenario, however, appears to have dispensed with the need for design specialists. Designers are the people who, in the traditional project, are responsible for defining the database and designing the system. They identify and specify what facilities the system is to offer to the end user, how these facilities will be structured, and precisely what each of them will do.

The fast-track approach also brings changes to these systems development roles. CASE tools can now provide normalized database designs from entity relationship models and default system architectures and facilities specifications from Business Function Models. This means that the business analyst can proceed to implementing the early versions of the required system without the input of database designers or application architects. This stage of the life-cycle does however provide a very clear example of the difference between a disciplined, but fast-track approach, and a 'hell for leather, hack it and hope' approach.

Example:

Diverging User Interfaces

During the prototyping exercise at the training centre, the analysts confirmed that there are two discernible groups of users, the people who work on the front desk, and those who maintain essential information for the accommodation administration system but do not work on the front desk. These are housekeeping staff who know about the status, facilities and availability of rooms. In turn, the housekeeping staff need information from the front desk about check-ins and check-outs so that they can schedule their activities. These users share information, but they do not share many facilities, so the analysts divided into two teams and each team developed the prototype further for one of these groups.

A month later, when the two developments came together again to demonstrate to senior management – catastrophe. Each team had developed its own style of user interface. Each was acceptable to the specific users who had contributed to the prototyping exercise, but the divergence between them increased the documentation to be written and the training to be developed and it also confused those staff who would need to use both sub-systems. On top of that it looked messy and senior management started to ask whether this project was under control.

In fact, the differences between the two styles of user interface were eliminated in a few days, and the new common style was demonstrated to the original user participants, who saw no need for the change but were not displeased by the result. The standards were written up for future use and the analysts lost a week of valuable time and learned a hard lesson, which an experienced applications designer would have already known. Consistency of interface has tangible and intangible benefits for the usability of an application, and standards set beforehand are cheaper to apply than standards enforced after the event.

Clearly, although fast-track projects can move faster than traditional projects, there are still disciplines to be observed, and there are differences in the skills and tools needed and differences in the roles to be played. Fast-track is not an abandonment of CASE Method: it is an evolution, which in some circumstances is better adapted to the new tools and techniques that have emerged from newer technology. But, as with animal evolution, what is well adapted for one environment can be ill-adapted for another. In adopting a fast-track approach, we must be sure that we are adopting it for suitable projects.

What Makes a Fast-track Project?

There are some hints in the example discussed above which indicate where fast-track is not immediately applicable:

- where there are large numbers of users that need to be consulted, particularly if they are widely spread geographically, and it is not possible to identify a small representative group. It will be difficult to coordinate requirements and to get approval for solutions.

- where the developers are inexperienced in the technology and the approach, and where they do not have sufficient top cover from experts or sufficient time for training and learning before the project. They may find themselves making expensive mistakes.

- where the users are inexperienced in the business area (for example, a new venture) or are inexperienced in the technology (for example, all their existing systems are batch with reports). In these situations, the users may not be able to state the requirement consistently.

- when the requirements, particularly for integration with other systems, are constantly changing, because of an unstable situation or political influences. Each iteration of the solution is likely to be contradicted by a new and inconsistent requirement.

There are many circumstances in which it would appear that the risks are too great to use a fast-track approach, but part of the fast-track approach is to identify potential fast-track projects from apparently unpromising circumstances. Figure 1-7 below represents a matrix of project types. Some will naturally fall into one quadrant or another and the development strategy for those will be clear. However, it is usually possible to split large or complex projects into smaller, more manageable projects, or to isolate those aspects of the project which make them unsuitable for fast-track. In this way a large complex project can be broken down into a series of smaller projects which can be tackled by iterative development or timeboxing, or a combination of the two.

For example, where there is programming complexity for a simple requirement, such as integrating the 'swipe' machine in the hotel registration example, and the implementation is mostly not user-interface driven, then the benefits of an evolutionary approach are minimized. We could consider a timebox within the fast-track project.

Figure 1-7
Selecting Fast-track Projects

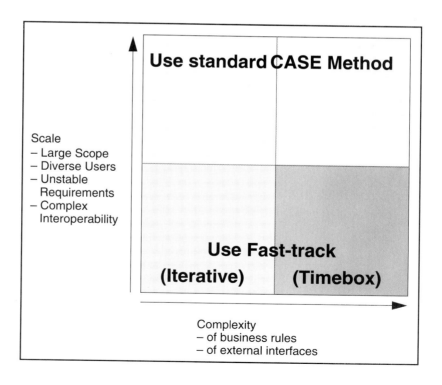

Figure 1-8 below develops from Figure 1-7 and indicates how an organization can, over a period of time, improve its capability to manage projects by fast-track techniques by effectively moving the internal divisions of the matrix. As developers' skills improve, bigger and more complex projects can be safely handled. As better technology is adopted and exploited, more can be done by business analysts, without recourse to ace programming teams in timeboxes.

Figure 1-8
Improving Fast-track Capability

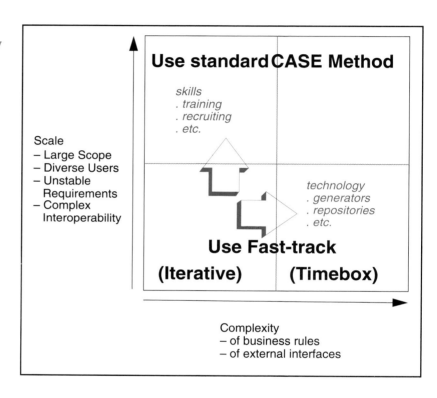

Fast-track
and CASE Tools

Fast-track is reliant on CASE tool support, both because CASE tool automation provides the most efficient way of performing development tasks and also because technology advances make new approaches possible. Throughout this book references are made to CASE tool support for the tasks and techniques discussed. Most of the comments and observations are applicable to a number of available CASE tools. The Oracle CASE tool set was used to develop the examples in this book and in the Tools and Techniques paragraphs of the task definitions, specific references are made to the appropriate facilities of the Oracle CASE tool set.

MANAGEMENT OF FAST-TRACK PROJECTS

**The Project
Development Life-cycle**

In CASE Method, as in all established systems engineering methods, the life-cycle of a development is divided into stages. The stages are then defined in terms of the tasks that need to be performed and the deliverables that will be produced within each stage. Figure 2-1 below illustrates this framework.

Figure 2-1

**The CASE Method
Life-cycle**

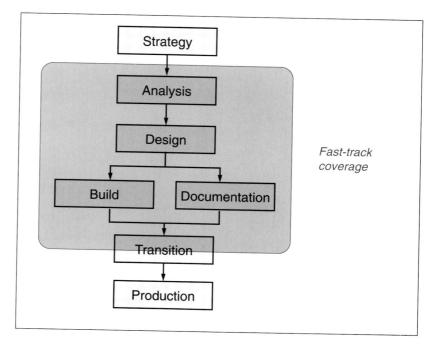

As we discussed in Chapter 1, the fast-track approach does not replace the CASE Method life-cycle. What it does is provide alternative techniques for use in some of the stages, namely analysis, design, build and documentation. When planning fast-track projects, we need to be aware of these boundaries and to be sure that we understand how our project integrates into the full life-cycle.

Fast-track Project Boundaries

The most critical factor for the success of a fast-track project is a clear and stable definition of the scope at the outset. The scope defines those processes or parts of processes that the system will support. The initial scoping **will not** specify the detailed requirements, but it **will** define the terms of reference for the project. The simplest starting point is from a predefined information systems strategy. Barker *et al.* (1990) define specific deliverables that should be available as the result of a comprehensive systems strategy. These represent the inputs for detailed analysis and subsequent implementation. The fact that some of the techniques applied in a fast-track project may differ from those used at the equivalent stage of a standard project, and indeed that the project stages themselves are redefined, does not alter the fact that if we do not have a clear statement of what is required and a statement of the context within which it is required to be delivered, then the project will be endangered from the start. This is true of all project planning, but particularly for fast-track projects where speed is of the essence. The strategic approach is very effective in setting project objectives and boundaries, but not all, or even most opportunities for fast-track come from a strategy plan. In *Thriving on Chaos* (Peters, 1987) Tom Peters majors on the need for responsiveness and innovation in business, prescribing small quick pilot projects in all areas of business, fostering what he calls a 'Small Starts' mentality. He says " *'Small Starts' then, is principally an attitude of hustling, testing and scrounging, aimed at shortening the development cycle by hook or by crook."* He is not talking specifically about information systems development, but if information systems development cannot be responsive in serving its customers, the operational divisions or departments of the enterprise, then how can those organizations be responsive to their customers? Many fast-track projects support just such organizations, and in those cases objectives must be set in less formal ways, perhaps through workshops and prototypes.

At the other boundary of the fast-track project, at the hand-over within the transition stage, careful attention is needed just as much, but for different reasons. Because end users have been directly involved in the development process throughout, the transition stage is in some ways simplified. For example, user training requirements may be less since the users are already familiar with the new system, and the acceptance test will be simpler since the user-visible parts of the system have already been extensively reviewed and tested by users as part of the development process. If we do not pay careful attention to the boundary hand-overs the productivity benefits of fast-track may be eroded by time spent in correcting errors caused because we did not understand the scope clearly before starting, or by duplicated effort in acceptance testing and user training.

Fast-track Stages

The fast-track approach exploits newly available technologies and techniques. To do this to best advantage, it is necessary to adopt a revision to the standard stages, blurring the distinctions between them in some cases and, as a result, redefining the roles of the project team members. Figure 2-2 shows how the difference in approach is reflected in different stage boundaries, although even so the boundaries are not hard and fast. Most of the requirements will emerge during scoping, but even during the build stage new requirements will emerge as the result of user reviews of partially completed components of the system. Likewise, the requirements process includes building a design prototype, and some components may have been prototyped even earlier.

Figure 2-2

The Fast-track Stages

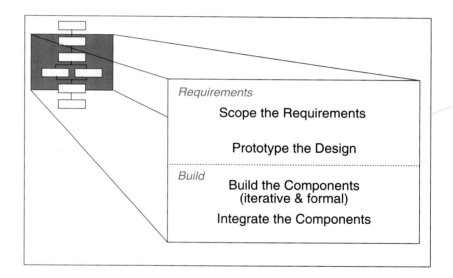

Requirements

This stage specifies the functional requirements of the proposed system and the overall structure of the system, the system architecture. Both of these will represent refinements of deliverables from the strategy stage, if there was a strategy stage. If the project is an isolated tactical development, then the first task of requirements specification is to set the boundaries of the development, in which case there may be additional work necessary to acquire the information that would otherwise have been inherited from the strategy.

Design Prototype

In the process of developing a system we must specify what the system needs to do (requirements analysis) and how the system needs to do it (design) before we build the system (implementation). By using code generator technology we can deliver a first-cut system directly from the requirements definitions. This provides a much more immediate way of reviewing the requirement with the users. If we have misunderstood the need, then our prototype will reveal that much more graphically than a formal specification, and, given the generator technology, much more quickly.

Iterative Build

In an iterative build the four original stages of analysis, design, build and documentation are somewhat blurred. The advantage is that the best way to ensure that a developer has understood precisely what a user wants is when the user can see the application that has been built. At that stage the user can much more easily identify shortcomings of the solution and will be more vividly reminded of factors that were forgotten when the requirement was originally specified. These changes can be incorporated in the next iteration and so the solution converges with the real user need. In addition, the user can specify interactively what help text, tutorial and reference documentation is required, as part of the review process. Typically, these will be only rough outlines, which will be fleshed out for the next review.

With a user-driven iterative build, it is only necessary to provide an overall definition of the requirements as the rest will emerge during the user reviews of each iteration of the proposed solution, but we can use iteration helpfully even for requirements that do not emerge from user review. It is often appropriate to use iterations to implement complex algorithmic processing. For example, we might implement a simplistic version of the processing to test the interfaces to other parts of the system and to test the database access, and implement the full complexity of the algorithm later. This approach simplifies the testing and debugging, and is well known and widely used in formal software development. In this book we use the term iterative development to mean user-driven development, and assume the above techniques are available and understood in the context of any formal build elements of fast-track projects.

Formal Build

Formal build is the approach to take when the design of the system component is going to be driven by some other constraint than the user interface and the right solution cannot easily be evolved from users reviewing and testing prototypes. For example, in the Guest Registration System, the interface to a credit card reader will be influenced primarily by the data interchange between the special device for reading cards and the screen processing software. The user interface impact is minimal. We still conduct user reviews during the build stage, but they tend to be shorter and the feedback tends to be to confirm or correct the implementation, rather than amplify the requirements, as happens in iterative development reviews.

Integration

During the build stage a number of sub-projects will have been conducted in parallel. Integration testing will be needed to bring these back together. This is analogous to the system test task in a classical life-cycle. We will see later that there are a number of precautions we can take at earlier stages of the project to ensure that the scale of this task is minimized.

Scoping the Project

Scoping is important in any project: in a fast-track project it is doubly important. Firstly, because there is less margin for error. A fast-track project will be over a shorter timescale (or it's not fast-track!) and so any overrun is proportionally more significant. This means that identifying the boundaries and the critical success factors for the project are vital activities.

Secondly, and more importantly, scoping is important because not all potential projects will benefit from a fast-track approach. A fast-track project uses specific tools and techniques to gain productivity. The project must be one where these are applicable. If, for example, the requirement is to satisfy a diverse user community which is spread over a wide geographic area, then an iterative build, based on frequent user reviews, would be impracticable. It would cost an unreasonable amount of time and money for the developer to tour the user locations for reviews, and what the first user requested the second user might veto, and so on. Conversely, if the users travel to the development location for reviews the cost is equivalent, or it may be even greater if we take into account possible lost opportunities to the business of having front-line staff away from their normal locations. Experience also shows that the technique of review/correct/prototype, which can work very well with a small group of people with a shared vision of the requirement, does not work with a large group of people with diverse views on the problem to be solved. Where there is no shared vision, the right approach is first to identify what the business or organization is trying to achieve, then what the best process is whereby it can achieve it, independently of how and whether it should be automated, and finally to specify and build the computer and organizational systems necessary to support it.

So to be most effective, fast-track projects not only need clear objectives and boundaries, they also need to have the right characteristics. But there are factors other than diversity and distribution of user population which will affect the risk associated with using a fast-track approach for a particular project. Figure 2-3 on page 20 identifies the most common factors affecting the risk level of a project. The objective in scoping a fast-track project is to ensure an acceptable risk level. A simple rule of thumb is to assign +1, 0 or –1 to each of the factors and to total the values: the higher the result, the riskier the project. But having assessed the risk we do not have to accept it or reject it; we can manipulate the risk level.

Figure 2-3

**Risk Factors in
a Fast-track Project**

Characteristic	Risk Factors
Project Content	Scale Complexity Stability External dependencies Technical dependencies
User Population	Diversity of views Geographical distribution Familiarity with technology Familiarity with application Motivation, morale, etc.
Project Team	Familiarity with fast-track Familiarity with application Motivation, morale, etc.
Project Environment	Dedicated resources Facilities, space, etc. Time Cost of failure CASE tools
Management	Commitment Familiarity with application Familiarity with fast-track

Example:

Phasing the Implementation

When they were prototyping the Guest Registration System at the training centre, it became apparent to the analysts that some of the users were happier than others in working with a prototype. It turned out that some of the hotels were keen to see a new system, while others were uneasy about changes in technology coming so soon after all the other changes caused by the acquisition. The analysts considered the risk factors of their project. They were happy about management commitment, which was reflected in support they had got in the project so far. They were happy about their own skills and tools. But the combination of a wide diversity of users spread over a wide geographical area, combined with some level of unease about the project among the user population, led them to suggest that the new Guest Registration System be developed for a subset of the hotels in the chain, concentrating on a smaller area, and including hotels from the parent chain and suitable representative hotels from the recently integrated chains. In this way the risk factors associated with the users were lowered considerably and the project was thought to be viable. It was noted that there might be a need for customization later, but the analysts felt that this was outweighed by the increased speed with which the whole process could be conducted.

In this example we see a project being scoped back to lower the risk so that it can be conducted more quickly, bringing operational benefits earlier, and providing a basis for a wider implementation later. This is a very typical fast-track approach, keeping the investment and risk down, gaining an early return on investment and then increasing the investment for a larger gain through enterprise-wide operation improvements later.

Partitioning the Project

At the outset we seek to identify projects, possibly by partitioning larger requirements. We can further optimize development of those projects by using iterative build and timeboxed formal build within the same project. If we can prioritize the functionality required, then a timebox can be applied. If a major component of the requirement is how it will appear and behave to the end user, then an iterative approach, based on user feedback, can be used. Figure 2-4 indicates how we can decide.

Figure 2-4

Strategies for Partitioning Fast-track Projects

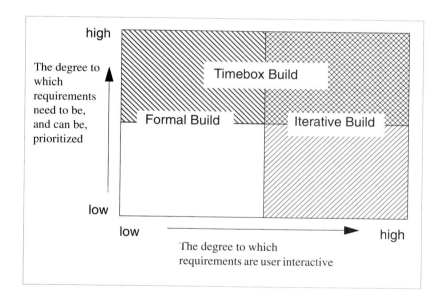

Figure 2-4 also indicates where formal build may still be required for some elements of a project and, of course, that a timebox may also be iterative.

Example:

Partitioning the Project

The Guest Administration System is to cover five main functional areas. These are illustrated by the function hierarchy shown in Figure 2-5 on page 22 which the analysts prepared. They are: Guest Registration,

Check-out, Room Status Information, Frequent Guest Programs and Corporate Accounts. Two analysts have been working on the early stages of the project. The team will be built up to five for the rest of the schedule. For the initial study, the two analysts worked together to model the overall data requirement in an entity relationship model, a function model (Figure 2-5) and a high-level dataflow diagram or context diagram which shows how the five functional areas link together.

The functionality required for Frequent Guest Programs and Corporate Accounts is specified by management policy. For this reason it is not planned to do an iterative build of these requirements (these will be timeboxed); the required functions from these two 'legs' of the hierarchy will be prioritized by management and one of the team will set to work on this with the target of implementing as much as possible from the list of requirements in three elapsed months. Three of the remaining team members will take the three remaining areas and the fifth will provide technical support to the team and handle any complex implementation requirements.

Figure 2-5

High-level Function Hierarchy of Guest Administration

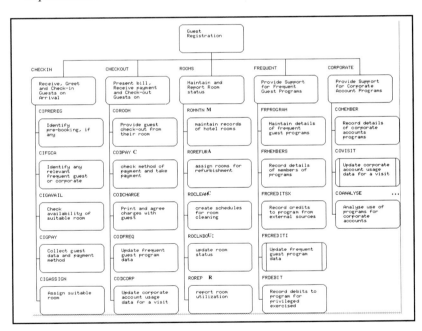

It was relatively easy to make the assignments in this case. We were helped by the fact that we had done an initial investigation and documentation of the requirements as a whole. This is an important point. Although partitioning allows us to conduct multiple 'mini-projects' in parallel, if they do not share a common view of the whole then problems will arise later. These will be of two kinds. The first relates to functionality, to what each partition should deliver. There will be instances where two developers clash over whose responsibility includes a particular subject area and there will be instances where two developers each think the other is responsible for a particular subject area. In one case we get duplicated effort; in the other, missing functionality in the delivered system. The second kind of problem relates to the use of the same information by more than one developer. In this case we can get conflicting definitions of data which can go undetected until the integration stage, by which time it will be expensive to resolve the conflicts. By spending some time modelling the requirement in a CASE tool (including building prototypes, as in this example), we have created a function model that defines the boundaries for each developer and we have defined a common information model (or entity model) which can help us to manage the shared data definitions by having a single common reference point.

Formal and Iterative Build within a Single Partition

In our example it was simple enough to create separate partitions for the iterative and the formal parts of the project. In many cases, what happens is that the partition is essentially user driven, but there are one or two areas where complex code may be required, for example, to specify a complex business rule formally. In these cases, rather than create multiple small partitions it is usually better to provide some time from an implementation specialist to develop just the complex customized code, within the same partition.

Cohesion and Coupling

The objective in defining the partitions is to provide work packages for the developers which they can complete in a reasonable timescale and which they can get on with largely independently of their colleagues. Two useful concepts that can be applied in this context are borrowed from Structured Design (Yourdon and Constantine, 1975). These concepts are Cohesion and Coupling and were originally defined to apply to program module designs but are equally applicable to a function hierarchy or part of it. Coupling, in its original definition, indicates the degree to which two modules share data or control information. Loose coupling is desirable and broadly means that the two modules only share database data, but are otherwise independent. Cohesion is a measure of the extent to which the internal parts of a module are related to one another. High cohesion is desirable and implies that the module is supporting a single complete process from start to finish.

Let us now apply these concepts to partitioning a function model in a fast-track project. Tight coupling between two partitions implies that two developers would be very dependent on each other. They would be constantly interrupting each other's work or becoming blocked waiting for the other to complete a vital task. Low coherence seems less dangerous, since it only implies that the developer has to divide her or his attention between relatively unconnected functions. This may be distracting, but provided the total volume of work is not too great, it should not be detrimental to progress. However, factors other than the function being carried out and the data being used can also have a bearing. In iterative build, user involvement is vital, not just for formal review sessions, but for informal discussions in between. If the same user is working with more than one developer, the interaction grows to a level that can easily become unacceptable to the user, who then gives less than full attention to either developer and the quality of the final deliverables slip. Conversely, if the same developer has to work with different users, then productivity slips, because we may need two or more separate review sessions for each iteration, and we can no longer use a single telephone call or short meeting to deal with as many issues.

For the purpose of project partitioning, we should find that the level of coherence increases and the level of coupling decreases if a partition serves only one user. A well-defined partition will have low coupling and high cohesion, so a single user is the optimum. In Chapter 4 we will examine what techniques and tools are available to a project manager in defining partitions.

Estimating in Fast-track Projects

Estimating is based on the expectation that history repeats itself. The same job should take the same resource the same time, in theory. In practice it is rarely exactly the same job and, if only because of the additional experience, it is rarely the same resource.

Top-down and Bottom-up Estimating

Estimating can be done top down or bottom up. An example of a top-down approach is Function Point Analysis (see Symons, 1991). In Function Point Analysis (FPA) we count aspects of the project that contribute to its size. These include, amongst others, numbers of inputs and outputs. Function Point Analysis also identifies a number of environmental and complexity factors that will affect the project, and applies weightings to the estimate on the basis of these factors. The advantage of top-down estimating is that it can be done early in the project: it requires less detailed information, and can quickly provide a 'ball-park' figure for budgetary purposes which can be refined at the beginning of a subsequent stage when more information exists.

Bottom-up estimating, also known as task-by-task estimating, is based on being able to estimate the effort for each task, and summing these to arrive at a total for the project. The advantage is that the estimates can be much more precise, and because they exist at a finer granularity they can be used for controlling and managing the project day by day. They cannot, however, be used to estimate a project from the outset because the precise task list and the scope of each task cannot be known in advance.

Timebox Estimating

Top-down and bottom-up estimating seek to provide as precise a figure as possible for the resources required to complete a defined deliverable, whether it be a design specification, a working module or whatever. We have already discussed above the difficulty in producing this, either precisely enough or early enough. Timebox estimating circumvents the problem by fixing the resources and allowing the deliverable to vary. Provided that we can prioritize the contents of the deliverable and can create a viable trade-out list (see "Managing Timebox Projects" on page 27), we can then use timeboxes to escape from the estimating dilemma. However, in order to create a realistic timebox project, which can at least deliver all the mandatory elements of the requirement, we do need a budgetary estimate, probably based on a top-down approach.

All estimating approaches are based on history: if we have no record of history, or no relevant experience to draw on, it becomes impossible to estimate. And because environmental factors, dependent on the particular organization and its people, have such an effect, it is not possible to take others' experience and expect it to apply, without adjustment, to our own projects. The corollary of this is that when a project is complete, one of the most valuable deliverables, not for the project itself but for future projects, is the completed project control documentation: what was planned and what was done; what was the estimated cost and what was the actual cost. Only with this information, gathered over a number of projects over time, can an organization build for itself an accurate estimating database.

Controlling Formal, Iterative and Timebox Builds

Formal, Iterative and Timebox builds need radically different management approaches if they are to succeed. In Chapter 4 we will see how these are implemented, but first we need to identify exactly what their differences are.

Managing Formal Build Projects

Formal build, described by Barker *et al.* (1990), follows the approach, which is now becoming a standard in the industry, of deliverable-oriented project management. In deliverable-oriented projects, the manager defines the deliverables which, if they are produced, will result in the project succeeding. If the task is to code and test a large program from a specification, then the required deliverables might include documented source code, test plans, test results, updated CASE repository, and so on. Then the project manager defines the tasks that need to be done to create those deliverables. Those tasks will normally be well known within the context of a particular development methodology, hence a project plan can be easily created with control points and quality assurance based on the deliverables themselves. Most methodologies identify interim deliverables which are not necessary for final success, but which identify milestones through the project. As the interim deliverables are produced and quality assured the project manager can establish that the project is on course. The test plan in the example above would be one such interim deliverable. We do not need to deliver a test plan in order to code and test a program successfully, but, particularly for a more junior developer, it will help the project manager to know that the project is proceeding satisfactorily if he or she can see that a comprehensive test plan has been produced before the code is written.

Managing Iterative Build Projects

In iterative build projects we can specify the deliverables, just as for formal build projects. It is more difficult to specify the interim deliverables, because in iterative build all the deliverables emerge, in skeletal form, early in the development and then evolve to their final form through a series of iterations, or repetitions, of a cycle of developing, reviewing and correcting. For example, if the project manager expects that three iterations through the cycle should be enough, based on experience, how can he or she tell, after one or two cycles, that the development is on target? Clearly there is no completed interim deliverable that can be examined and quality checked on which to make a judgement.

The project manager needs a way of measuring progress, but cannot rely on the deliverables themselves: in an iterative build these are always changing until the project is complete. What the manager can rely on is that the rate of change of the deliverables ought to be decreasing. Each iteration should bring the development closer to completion, should bring the deliverables closer to maturity, should result in fewer changes, and in this lies the seed of a useful metric. If at each review we count the number of changes required by the user, we should see that number decrease over time, and if we have an expectation, based on experience, of what the rate of decrease should be, we can measure progress of iterative build projects by using a piece of information which is easily gathered, namely, the number of change requests at each review. In general, the rate of change tends to resemble the curve in Figure 2-6. In fact, the number of changes may never quite reach zero no matter how many iterations we go through because there is often a tendency to try new, but unnecessary, variations. If, however, the curve resembles that in Figure 2-6, the project manager can rest easy (if a project manager ever rests easy).

Figure 2-6

Required Changes versus Iterations

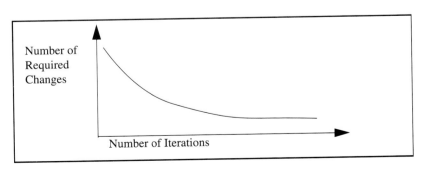

Managing Timebox Projects

The essence of a timebox project is that the deliverables are not known at the outset, or rather, of the deliverables specified, it is not known which will finally be completed in the available time (see "Timeboxing" on page 6). The internal conduct of a timebox development may be formal or iterative, but because there may not be time to complete all the requirements it is necessary to prioritize them so that the team can spend their limited resources on delivering the features and functions that have the most value to the user. As the project proceeds, circumstances change. For example, a particular feature takes longer to implement than was expected, or the review of a development iteration reveals new features, more desirable than some already known. When this happens it will be necessary to reprioritize the outstanding work. Figure 2-7 shows one way of assigning priorities, the so-called MoSCoW (**M**ust have, **S**hould have, **C**ould have, **W**on't have) model. Each requirement can then be evaluated against these classes and assigned an appropriate priority. The project plan should allow for short meetings to review and re-assign priorities. For an iterative timebox these should be held as part of the design prototype review and then at least once during build. In either case the plan should allow time for additional review meetings to be scheduled should the need arise.

Figure 2-7

Classification of Priorities

Classification	Meaning
Must Have	This item will be included in the delivered project.
Should Have	The current project plan indicates that this item will be included. If circumstances alter, it may be traded out (see next classification).
Could Have	The current project plan indicates that this item will not be included. If circumstances alter it may be traded in (see previous classification).
Won't Have	This item will not be included in the delivered project.

Quality Management in Fast-track Projects

Quality management in fast-track projects is no different from that in any other project, nor any less important. The difference lies in the need to maintain productivity and speed. We have less room to manoeuvre than on some occasions. How does this affect the way we plan and execute quality assurance?

There is a story in ancient Chinese Taoist literature of a famous doctor, known throughout the land for his success at restoring to health many patients thought to be at death's door. His brother was also a doctor but little known outside his own village. A great lord was discussing his profession with the famous doctor, who insisted that his brother was a better physician than himself. The explanation for this surprising assertion was as follows: *"I have had some success at curing serious illness, and am well known for it: my brother is a far superior diagnostician who detects and cures serious illness before it manifests itself, hence no one knows of his success. I am famous because I am less skilled than he."*

The same is frequently true in the information technology industry; some great reputations have been made in defect correction. The objective of quality management, however, must be to minimize the need for such skills by anticipating likely problems and either circumventing them or detecting and correcting them early, before they become apparent and critical.

Repeatable Processes

Quality assurance is not the same as quality checking. Regardless of what quality checking we do, if the processes we perform are repeatable and always produce the same deliverables in the same time with the same resource usage, then we have much greater assurance of the quality. What we mean by the process is the definition of the tasks, the deliverables, the techniques to be applied to perform the tasks, the resources required and the tools to be used. When a project plan is made up of standard tasks that are well known and understood and where the project team is familiar with the techniques and tools associated with each task, the risk of unacceptable quality is lower. In information systems development, unlike many manufacturing and clerical processes, every project has its uniquenesses. The role of quality management is to identify, minimize and isolate the unique aspects of each project and to identify additional quality measures and additional measurement points to provide early warning of problems in these specific areas.

If a task is non-standard, it is less likely that we can predict it safely. Also, the larger the scale of a task, the more likely it is to confound our predictions, even if, in principle, it is a standard task. Ask me to juggle three oranges for half a minute, and I will do so with confidence. Ask me to juggle them for five minutes and we can expect some bruised fruit. The risk of failure increases in two dimensions, with scale and with the degree of non-standardness; Figure 2-8 opposite illustrates how. This means that we cannot always have predictably repeatable processes, so we are forced to add quality checking after the event to test whether the performance of a particular task was successful. To do this we have to identify the points at which we are going to introduce the quality checks.

Figure 2-8

The Risk to Repeatability

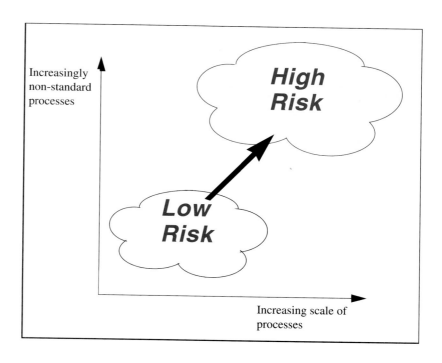

Quality Check Milestones

Milestones in projects are there to tell us that we are making progress. A milestone is usually the completion of a task or a deliverable, but we need to be sure that it represents real progress. There is no value in ticking items off the 'to do' list just to make ourselves or management feel good if we will have to go back and do them again later. When we reach a milestone we need to assure ourselves (and our sponsor) of the quality of the job done or the deliverable produced. They have to be not just deliverables, but 'acceptables'. We may group a number of small tasks or deliverables together to represent one milestone and make that the object of quality checking. We may need to break down large tasks and define interim milestones to ensure that the process is being conducted satisfactorily. The challenge in setting the milestones is deciding what is 'big' and what is 'small' but the size of a task is relative to the timescale of the project and the degree of slippage which can be accommodated without risk. In a fast-track project the milestones are probably at the end of each stage plus one or two more during the build stage to guide iterations and to reprioritize timeboxes.

Quality Measures
and Acceptable Quality

The processes tell us how to produce the right deliverables in the right way, and the milestones identify the points at which we will check the processes. To do this effectively and efficiently we need to know how we will measure quality, and what level will be regarded as satisfactory. CASE tools can provide detailed analysis of deliverables that are represented in the repository.

Example:
The Scoping Workshop

Having completed a scoping workshop the analysts documented what they know so far of the requirements. The statement of scope evolved in the workshop with user management, so it is acceptable. Before it can be regarded as acceptable for use in the next stage, the team need to check that the documentation is consistent and complete. They do this by running a series of quality checks which are part of the CASE tools. These show that one of the entities (Block Booking) is not used by any business function, that is, we had not specified what processing is required to deal with block bookings. This is because at the workshop nobody could say for sure what was wanted. It was agreed that this should be subject to more investigation and if it turned out to be a big job, it should not hold up the rest of the project.

As well as knowing what we are going to check and how, we need to know what is acceptable. In the example above it was 'no exceptions except where justified by project circumstances'. The milestone report would include the explanation of why the entity *Block Booking* was not properly documented.

Quality Roles

In a fast-track project it is unlikely that there would be a single quality representative or quality manager. The team would normally be too small to justify that degree of specialization and, in any event, quality is everyone's responsibility. The project manager and senior team members will take most responsibility for planning, but quality checking activities should be shared to promote team working and to improve communication among the team.

Contingency

There is no point in performing any quality checking activities if there is no time to correct any defects discovered. The project plan should include time for defect correction, and the quality plan should include an indication of the correction method for any measure that is used and an indication of the likely scale of rework.

Summary

Fast-track projects are like any other projects: they need planning, monitoring and managing. They differ from traditional software development projects because the established mechanisms and techniques for project management are not always applicable. In this chapter we have looked at some of these differences and identified appropriate techniques and mechanisms to support the fast-track approach. In Chapter 4 and subsequent chapters we will look in more detail at how these techniques are incorporated into a project.

Chapter

3

FAST-TRACK TECHNIQUES

Fast-track projects maintain a strong emphasis, indeed a reliance on iteration and the evolution of deliverables from early prototypes. Figure 3-1 below illustrates this approach and indicates how workshops, prototypes and evolutionary development replace the more formal techniques and deliverables of the traditional approach.

Figure 3-1
The Fast-track Approach

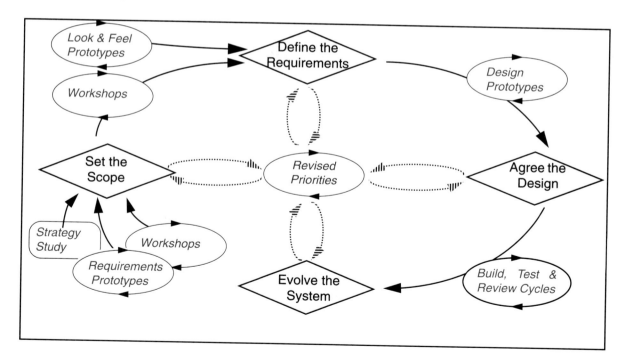

The previous chapter discusses how project management of fast-track projects differs from the management of more traditional style projects. This chapter is concerned with the differences in the conduct of fast-track projects, where the tasks to be done call for different techniques or for novel applications of existing techniques. Many techniques used in fast-track projects, such as entity relationship modelling, are well known from CASE Method and other sources. Some of the techniques, however, are specific to fast-track, or their application in fast-track projects is sufficiently specialized that it is worth describing the fast-track variant in some detail. This chapter introduces the techniques, provides an overview and discusses their applicability to fast-track. Later chapters describe the use of the techniques in specific tasks at the various stages of the life-cycle.

General Professional Skills

Interpersonal Skills

Successful systems development has always required a high level of skill in dealing with people, be this in interviews, feedback sessions, prototype reviews, progress meetings or just informally in the project office. Fast-track is no different, except that **all** the team members will need these skills. The old days of the 'back-room boys' are gone. If we want to be responsive to the needs of our customers, we have to be able to talk to them, and make ourselves understood. Interpersonal skills, or 'people skills', can be taught and learned, and they must be practised. But it is also true to say that not everyone has the same aptitude. Many of the techniques used in fast-track and in other CASE Method projects make use of specific interpersonal skills: for example, in feedback sessions, workshops and reviews, all of which are discussed below and in other books in this series.

Leadership and Management Skills

Leadership is a vital ingredient of fast-track projects. Because change and urgency are day-by-day companions of a fast-track project manager a 'play it by the book' approach (even this book) will not be enough. The successful fast-track project manager will blend a strong focus on results with a flexible and resourceful approach to getting them. Traditionally, project managers are strong on results focus and less strong on the more visionary approach associated with leadership. The popular image of a project manager is more likely to be poring over the details of a test plan than waxing lyrical over the long-term benefits of user-driven software development. But in organizations that are adopting a new approach, such as fast-track, there will be a need for the leader as well as the manager, even though there is a tension between the two viewpoints. The need to welcome this tension and exploit it rather than try to avoid it is explored graphically by Craig Hickman in his fascinating book *Mind of a Manager, Soul of a Leader* (Hickman, 1990).

Test Planning and Testing

Preparing and using test plans is an essential part of development. Everyone knows it must be done, but it is difficult to find an example test plan or even a helpful definition of what should go in one.

Planning

A test plan consists of a series of test cases, scenarios, to be tested together with an indication of the expected outcome and success criteria. A test case may be single step:

> *Test a customer query dialogue to ensure that it will support searches on partial addresses.*

The success criterion might be to return a search on 'High Street' in 5 seconds or less.

Or it may be a multi-step test case:

> *Test a multi-page screen dialogue to ensure that we can respond to a customer's request for the status of an order, given only the customer name and the approximate date of the order, then print/fax the status to the customer.*

The sooner you start to develop test scenarios the better. They provide useful example data for user reviews and they provide a more objective source of testing than usually emerges in the user reviews. Of course, where code generators are used what we are testing is not the code itself; we assume that if we have asked for data validation against a set of valid values, the generated code will perform that validation correctly. What we are testing is the **design**. Have we got the correct set of valid input values? Is this the point at which they are entered and checked?

There are simple guidelines that can help you create test plans:

- A multi-step test case will be made up of several simpler cases, which themselves may be made up of still simpler and single-step cases, as in the examples above.

- Each test case needs suitable data to exercise it and test data should be reused for multiple test cases where there are common steps embedded.

- Each test plan should comprise only the set of test cases necessary to establish that the object of the test does what it is supposed to do, nothing else.

- The object of a test scenario, or a series of scenarios, may be a single module, a group of modules making up a partition of a system under development, or indeed the whole system.

It is impossible to test all possible behaviour of even a relatively simple system in a **short** timescale and with **reasonable** effort, where short and reasonable are measured in terms of the cost and benefits normal in commercial data processing. Successful test planning is about ensuring that as much as possible is covered in the available time, and no significant errors remain. The best way to build a test plan is by working from the simple towards the complex, by analogy, from test cases for expected inputs (the simple) to unexpected inputs (the complex) and from simple structural rules, such as whether the right customer details are retrieved, to complex processing, such as whether the interest charges on overdue payments are correctly calculated.

Figure 3-2 below summarizes the five different test scenario types and their objectives. All scenarios should include tests to ensure that the facility does perform correctly given the expected inputs, and also that it performs correctly when given unexpected inputs: for example if data validation fails, is the exception processing appropriate and are error messages informative enough for the user to be able to diagnose and correct the error?

Figure 3-2
Test Scenario Types

Rule Types	Test Objectives
Structure	Ensure the facility is invoked in the way required. Ensure that it expects and gets any input parameters and shared data. Ensure that it is not accessible by unauthorized users, and not invokable through prohibited routes.
Reusable Data	Where the module is responsible for data definitions, ensure that all rules have been encoded correctly and that exceptions are dealt with correctly.
Specific Data	For all module-specific data rules, ensure they have been correctly encoded and that exceptions are dealt with correctly.
Complex Processing	Ensure expected and unexpected inputs to all complex processing rules are handled. Ensure that data-driven navigation is managed as required and is acceptable to house standards and end users.
Documentation	Ensure accurate and informative help and hint messages are included throughout.

We can create simple structural scenarios directly from the requirements models: for example, which business units require access to which facilities. These may become more complex once the 'look and feel' rules have been applied and we have navigation between pages, windows and modules. We can construct data scenarios from the data definitions. There is no point in data definition tests being repeated by every module that uses the data. One partition should be responsible for testing a set of data definitions. This is usually the partition responsible for the initial creation of the data, often as part of a data maintenance and housekeeping subsystem. Where these definitions are reused elsewhere we can then assume they are managed correctly, and the modules that reuse them should only test additional rules specific to those modules. The last tests are those that relate to more complex processing: for example, calculations or navigation based on data values.

A test plan will not necessarily have each of these five sections, nor will it necessarily cover all the tests in the order listed. The list is a guide, a starting point in preparing a test plan. Figure 3-3 below shows a fragment of a simple test scenario. It may seem an onerous task to create detailed test plans in a fast-track project; however, the level of detail can be varied according to the extent to which the requirement is not obvious to the developer and users, and the test scenarios will be reused as 'scripts' for conducting user reviews.

Figure 3-3
An Example Test Plan Layout

Step	Action	Expected Result	Notes
1	Re-create test database from SQL script	Initial start-up data loaded	Script drops the tables if they already exist. If not, will display 'table does not exist' errors; ignore them
2	Enter new guest record: Name: *Smith* Forename: *David* Company: *n/a* Payment: *Visa* ...	Record is acceptable and committed	Make a note of the system assigned Guest id. It will be used in step 5
3	Repeat step 2 and request duplication of 'David Smith' on warning message	System issues warning message 'guest already known'	Tests for uniqueness on guest name, but will allow if requested after warning message
4	...		

Test scenarios can be managed in Oracle CASE tools as documents. These can then be cross-referenced to the modules, tables and so on that are referenced in the scenario. Figure 3-4 on page 36 shows an example of this technique.

Figure 3-4
Test Scenarios and Modules

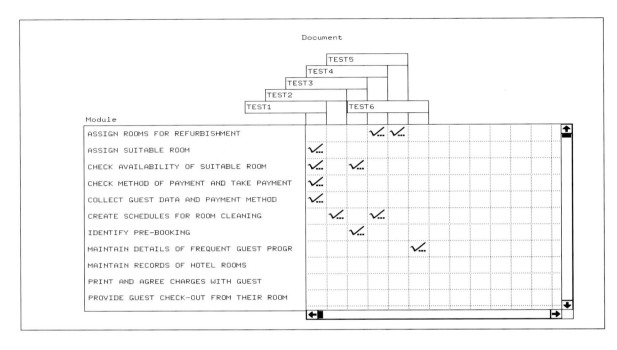

Testing

At test time the scenario documents we have prepared will drive the activity. The results can be recorded either as revisions to the test plan (say in another column) or in a separate test results document which would substitute the notes column in Figure 3-3 for an actual result column, as in Figure 3-5 opposite. The advantage of this approach is that the test plan is preserved for reuse, and the test results document can be cross-referenced to modules, tables and so on that need reworking as a result of the test. We can even use different values to indicate *tested ok* and *tested, needs reworking* in the cross-reference.

Just as we can manage the test scenarios as documents in Oracle CASE tools, we can also manage the results in the same way. Figure 3-6 opposite shows an example.

Figure 3-5
An Example Test Results Layout

Step	Action	Expected Result	Actual Result
1	Re-create test database from SQL script	Initial start-up data loaded	OK
2	Enter new guest record: Name: Smith Forename: David Company: n/a Payment: Visa ...	Record is acceptable and committed	Guest id returned: '**100123**'
3	Repeat step 2 and request duplication of 'David Smith' on warning message	System issues warning message 'guest already known'	Refused to allow duplicate David Smith ****ERROR****
4	...		

Figure 3-6
A Matrix of Test Results against Module

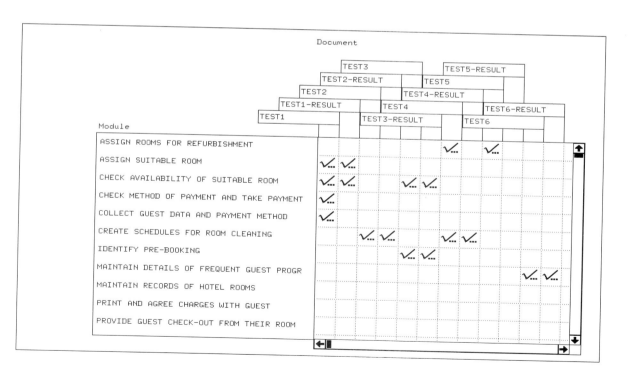

CASE Method Techniques

Objective Setting

Success can only be measured against objectives or goals achieved. If a project has no objectives, then it can be difficult to establish that the project has succeeded, and it can be difficult for the participants to know what is expected of them. A project will not have been initiated unless someone, probably the project sponsor, has some idea what the project is intended to achieve. One of the first steps of the project planning stage is to clarify and agree these objectives. Project objectives are of two kinds, Functional objectives, and Management objectives. Functional objectives indicate which business processes are to be supported, what business events the system should respond to and what key results the system should produce. Management objectives indicate the expected costs and timescale and there may be other management objectives such as utilization of resources, or contribution to larger business objectives, for example, cost reduction in the end-user department. Estimates of costs and time will need to be revised and refined during the planning stage and beyond, but an initial objective should be set to provide a framework for more detailed plans. How these initial objectives map onto the project can be seen in Figure 3-7 below.

Figure 3-7
Project Objectives

Type	Description	Project Impact
Management	Cost	Resource Plan
	Time	Schedule
Functional	Business Processes	Function Decomposition Model
	Events	System Architecture Model
	Key Results	System Architecture Model

Information Modelling

A complete definition of the information used in a system includes not only the traditional elements, based on the entity relationship modelling, but also the enrichment of that definition to include constraints and other invariant rules that always apply whenever a particular data element is used. One widely used type of invariant is the referential integrity constraint: for example, *'No guest record can be deleted if there is an associated outstanding booking'*.

An information model exists at two levels:

- Firstly the entity relationship model created in business analysis, where the definitions relate to abstract concepts of the information used in an organization.

- Secondly the logical schema model created in design where the model defines a possible implementation, but details such as which tables are to be clustered together to improve access times, or whether a particular business rule is to be enforced in the database (server side) or in the applications (client side) are not specified.

It is not unusual for there to be multiple levels of refinements within these two levels; however, for fast-track projects two levels will normally suffice except that in implementation we may distinguish between the logical design and an optimized physical design:

- The physical database schema can be regarded as a refinement of the logical schema tuned to a specific intended implementation. This would then reflect features of the chosen implementation database, for example the use of clustered tables in an Oracle database.

The entity relationship model specifies the structure and structural rules of the information model. The logical schema model also includes constraints, such as column validation, column derivation rules, table constraints and referential integrity constraints, which can be implemented automatically by the Oracle Generators if they are documented at the design or system level (on tables and columns). If they are documented at the analysis or business level (entities and attributes) as free text, they are not all automatically transformed into code by the Oracle Generators. This means that the best way to model information requirements so that redundant effort is eliminated is to capture what can be captured at analysis first and then move to the database design as soon as possible. This is a pragmatic approach that we will see mirrored in function and architecture modelling. Our primary aim is efficiency and the elimination of redundancy.

As part of information modelling we will identify invariant validation rules for individual data items (formalized in design as column constraints) and constraints that apply between more than one data item (formalized as table constraints). When we implement the database design, and subsequently implement the modules that use the database, we must decide where the constraints are to be enforced. In traditional programming we have no choice: business rule enforcement is part of the application code; however, with the advances in database-server technology and client/server development tools, we have the option to implement business rules in the database server. This has the advantage that no program can corrupt the database. It has the disadvantage that the user interface may be less friendly if no rules, including simple validation, are enforced until the transaction is committed to the database. To overcome this, part of the database design process is to decide whether business rules should be enforced on the server side, the client side or both. The basis of the decision is a balance of usability (which suggests that all rules be client side), system optimization (which dictates that everything should only be done once) and database integrity (which dictates that all rules should be done in the database server).

Figure 3-8 below illustrates these levels and the major elements that go to make them up.

Figure 3-8
The Information Model

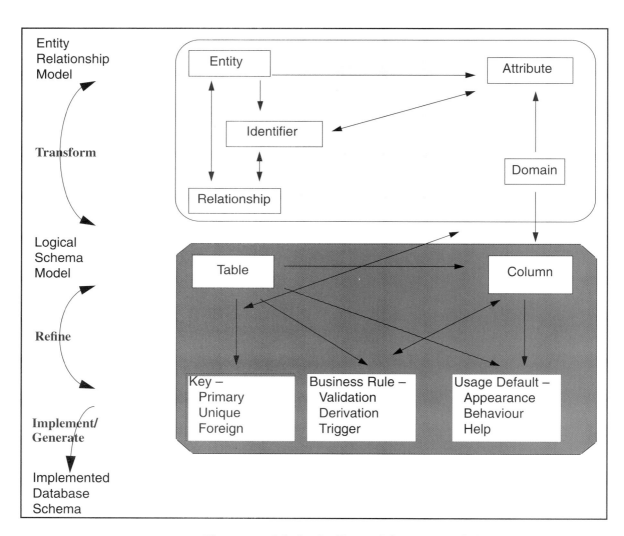

The usage defaults in Figure 3-8 are part of the data definitions: for example, room status is stored as a single character Occupied, Free or Unavailable, but it is always displayed as a poplist. The usage default (poplist) is not necessary information for generating the database schema; it will be used in generating the client-side applications. Nonetheless, it is specified as part of the data definition, once, and then inherited by every client-side application that uses the data.

Information modelling is not an isolated activity, it is part of the whole project development process. As our understanding grows, so too do the models of that understanding – the information model, the function model and the architecture model. This means that we return to the information model throughout the development, adding to it, correcting it, refining it. Figure 3-9 below shows how information modelling using the Oracle CASE tools fits into the fast-track project life-cycle and identifies the tasks and stages, where these modelling activities are defined in detail.

Figure 3-9
Oracle CASE Information Modelling

Chapter Stage/Sub-stage	Task	Modelling Activity
Planning Stage (see Chapter 4)	Task 1: *Scope – by feedback* Task 2: *Scope – by workshop*	Outline the entity model
Requirements Definition (see Chapter 5)	Task 3: *Prepare for and conduct requirements workshops*	Detail the entity model
Design Prototype (see Chapter 5)	Task 6: *Create default database design*	Transform entity model to logical schema Add business rules to logical schema Add look and feel defaults (usage defaults) to logical schema Add physical schema definitions to logical schema
Iterate Build and User Review (see Chapter 6)	Task 5: *Collate external changes*	Revise and refine logical schema definitions
Design Prototype (see Chapter 5)	Task 9: *Generate design prototype*	Transform physical schema into implemented database(s)
Iterate Build and User Review (see Chapter 6)	Task 5: *Collate external changes*	Revise elements of logical schema and reimplement
Performance Trials (see Chapter 7)	Tuning	Optimize and document elements of the database schema

Function Modelling

Function modelling, sometimes known as activity modelling or process modelling, specifies firstly what the user organization does or plans to be doing. This is the business function model and it is expressed in business terminology. Secondly, function modelling specifies what the system needs to do to support the user organization. *CASE*Method Function and Process Modelling* (Barker and Longman, 1993) discusses function modelling and architecture modelling in great depth. In fast-track projects a simpler view of function modelling is usually sufficient. Figure 3-10 below shows the component parts of a fast-track function model, and just as with the information model, the function model evolves throughout the project: we gather information at the time it is available and needed and record it in the most efficient way.

Figure 3-10
The Function Model

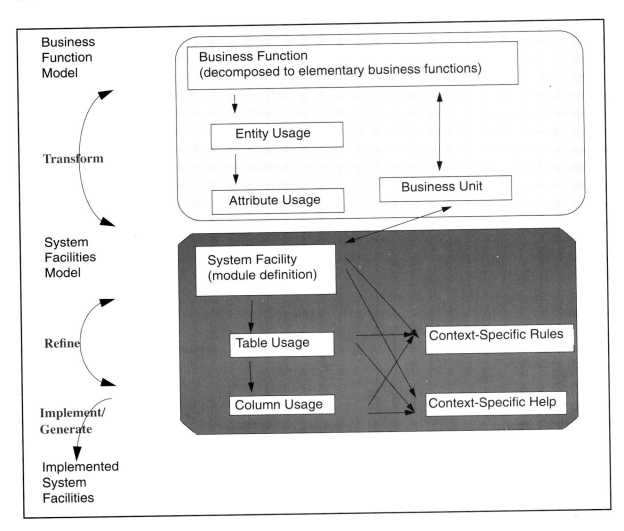

At the scoping stage the functions identified are unlikely to be elementary business functions. Two or, at a maximum, three levels of decomposition should be enough to set scope at the outset, and no detailed usages of entities and attributes need be specified. Typically, dataflow models are used to represent context, normally only one level. If the users in the scoping workshop prefer the use of dataflow diagrams to function decomposition, then you may have all the decomposition represented in dataflow diagrams; there is no great difference either way at this stage. Any dataflows and datastores defined at this time can be regarded as indicative only, and not definitive. Using a dataflow diagram sometimes helps users who are thinking in terms of a sequence of activities linked by the passing of data. Using a function decomposition can help by allowing the participants to concentrate on what needs to happen, without being tempted to think in terms of the current procedures and sequences. Whichever approach is more comfortable for the participants is the better one.

In the requirements stage the decomposition needs to be completed to the elementary business function level and the data usages specified. My preference is not to use multi-levelled dataflow models, but to decompose the functions individually and then identify the data usages at the elementary level only. It is rarely very helpful to draw dataflow models of data maintenance functions or reporting functions, but for transactional functions, where the sequence from initial external event to the final result involves several elementary functions, dataflow diagrams or function dependency diagrams show transactional sequence more clearly than function hierarchies. The Oracle CASE tools provide facilities to pursue functional analysis either way to produce the same deliverables. The style described here is the one that maximizes the potential of the CASE toolset to assist. The guiding principle is pragmatism, so we must balance our personal preferences against the degree of automation and assistance that the CASE tools provide to one approach or the other.

Application Design

Application design is the process of transforming the business function model into the specification of individual computer-based facilities (or modules or programs) that support the functions identified. The design process also specifies how these facilities are linked together and accessed by users as a whole system. This is treated as a separate activity under "Systems Architecture Modelling" on page 44. Although the two activities are carried out together and use much of the same information (the business function model), they use different techniques and produce different deliverables.

We can now concentrate on designing a specific facility, one or more modules, to support a specific elementary business function. The Oracle CASE tools provide a utility that transforms elementary function definitions into appropriate module definitions, mapping function, entity usage and attribute usage onto facility, table usage and column usage. This utility – see the section on "Default Application Design" in *Oracle CASE*

Dictionary Reference Manual (Oracle Corporation, 1994a) – will create one module to support more than one function, if they are sufficiently similar, and will create modules of different types (screen, report, etc.) according to the processing requirements of the function. The module designs created are defaults. In some cases they will be perfectly adequate as they stand; in other cases they will need to be modified, probably after user review.

What it can do, the toolset will do more quickly and more accurately than a human. What it cannot do is apply genuine intelligence. Once again the principle of the fast-track approach is to use the tools to take the error prone drudgery out of development tasks and use human expertise only on those tasks that the machine cannot automate. In this way we can design a complete system very quickly, and then use our skills and experience, driven by user input, to complete the process.

Usability Design

Usability is that quality of a system that makes it easy to learn, easy to use, and encourages the user to regard the system as a positive help in getting the job done. Experience indicates the usability in a system comes from:

- consistency – because we can quickly reapply what we have learned, from any tool or application in the environment.

- predictability – because when, as inevitably it must, exceptions occur or something goes wrong, we know how the system will behave. This is effectively consistency applied to the unexpected!

- flexibility – because as the requirements change we want the user interface to be able to change gradually: a small change in requirements should not require a revolutionary new interface.

The right time to start thinking about usability is before we start design. If we want consistency and predictability then we need to set out rules that can be applied to all aspects of the design and that result in common appearance and behaviour throughout the system. These rules may already exist in an organization, but if not they need to be developed before we start to generate any applications code. Equivalent rules apply to the design of the architecture (see the next section). Once again, in fast-track, the objective is a simple approach, which will allow us to solve simple problems quickly and easily.

Systems Architecture Modelling

In a formal project the architecture model will be much more complex than could be represented in Figure 3-10 on page 42. For fast-track projects we can make a number of simplifying assumptions without increasing the risk. These simplifications decrease the work to be done and hence improve overall productivity. Much of the discussion on systems architectures in

Barker and Longman (1993) focuses on data distribution and the interconnection of sub-systems. It is the nature of a fast-track project that these aspects are less complex, so a fast-track architecture is more concerned with how the external events that the system must respond to, the results it must achieve and the business processes that it must support are mapped onto the components of the system solution. This enables us to specify a system structure to meet the business needs by ensuring that the facilities of the system are available to the right users and that facilities invoke other facilities to match the structure of events triggering functions.

System architecture is often thought of as part of design, which it is to some extent. But if the architecture is to reflect the real world accurately, then we must think about it earlier than that, and the Design Prototype will reflect the first-cut system architecture for the users' review, very early on in the process. It is unlikely that this first cut will be one hundred percent satisfactory, because it will have been constructed on only partial information. If it is to have any value, however, and not alienate the user, it ought to be based at least on the best information we have acquired at that point rather than being a complete shot in the dark. The Oracle CASE tools can create a default system architecture by transforming an extended business function model – see the sections on "Default Application Design" and "Default Menu Design" in *Oracle CASE Dictionary Reference Manual* (Oracle Corporation, 1994a). Although the architecture will need refinement, it is created automatically and provides a simple way of feeding back to the user an example or suggestion that will be more effective in provoking comment and correction than any amount of open-ended discussion about what might be possible or desirable.

As Figure 3-10 on page 42 shows, if we know which business functions are performed by which business units (groups of users), then we can surmise which facilities, designed to support those functions, will need to be accessible to which system users. This architecture will need to be refined to reflect facilities that must invoke others directly, rather than just through menus, and to specify security roles for users, if necessary.

The style guide in Figure 3-11 on page 46 represents the guidelines for the 'look and feel' of screen and report layouts. These are part of the project standards. They may be inherited from previous projects or from a departmental standard – the house rules. They will be needed before the design prototype if the appearance of the system is to be consistent. In the Oracle CASE toolset the style guide is encoded as a set of rules which the code generators obey, but which the developers can modify. If we agree a style guide with the users early on in the project these can be reused over and over, and only modified where necessary to meet a particular need (who said rules were for breaking – occasionally?).

Figure 3-11
The System Architecture Model

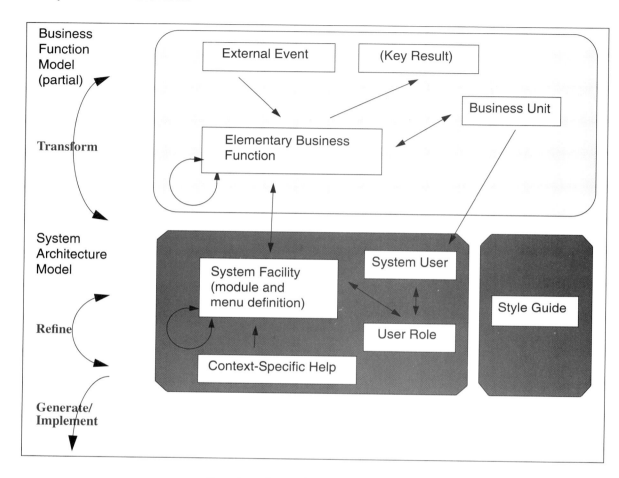

Security roles and access control do not usually reflect elements of the business function model so they can be treated as part of the system model. Direct invocation of one facility by another is best done at design time if there is no automatic transformation from function dependency to facilities invocation, which is the situation with most current CASE tools (including Oracle CASE). If it is done in the business function model, it will need to be redone later in the system architecture model. In a fast-track project we always seek to avoid redundant effort. Those who prefer to enhance the business function model with this information recommend it because that model is often a sign-off deliverable with the users and a hand-over document from analysts to designers. In a fast-track project, neither of these otherwise valid reasons holds. The design prototype, and the changes to it that have been requested, are the user sign-off deliverable. Since there is no internal division of labour in the team to necessitate an analysis to design hand-over, a more formal definition is not necessary.

The Function model and the Architecture model tend to evolve together. Figure 3-12 below shows how the different function and architecture modelling activities fit into the fast-track life-cycle.

Figure 3-12
Oracle CASE Function and Architecture Modelling

Chapter Stage/Sub-stage	Task	Modelling Activity
Planning Stage (see Chapter 4)	Task 1: *Scope – by feedback* Task 2: *Scope – by workshop* Task 3: *Scope – by prototype*	Produce a context diagram (top-level dataflow diagram) Define the functional scope
Requirements Definition (see Chapter 5)	Task 2: *Prototype look and feel requirements*	Define style guide
	Task 3: *Prepare for and conduct requirements workshops*	Complete the functional specification Dataflow model the transactional elementary functions Specify data usage of elementary functions Specify which business units carry out which elementary functions Specify events that trigger the elementary functions
	Task 7: *Create default application design*	Create a default application design
	Task 8: *Create default system architecture*	Create a default systems architecture design
	Task 10: *Review design prototype*	Define facility processing (Initial Specification)
Iterate Build and User Review (see Chapter 6)	Task 4: *Review system components with users*	Define and implement facility processing (Respecification)

Feedback Sessions

In a feedback session one group of people validate and correct their understanding of a subject by consulting the experts on that topic. The typical use in software development projects is for the development team to feed back their understanding of the system requirements to the sponsors of the development and other key users. This initial understanding may have been gained from interviews, from the developers' previous experience or from a previously developed model of the industry, sometimes called a template model. In a feedback session the presenter is trying to find out where his or her understanding is incorrect, and to get it corrected. This is unlike the situation where the presenter is trying to convince the audience that he or she already has all the answers.

The idea of conducting what is effectively a group interview in a presentation format is very successful at identifying and resolving conflicts and misunderstanding. The notes from a feedback session are usually in the form of corrections and annotations on the presentation materials used. These will need to be consolidated after the session, and the developers can then move on with a high degree of confidence that they understand what the users need and want. Figure 3-13 below shows the structure of a feedback sessioni and the steps leading to it and following it.

Figure 3-13
The Feedback Session

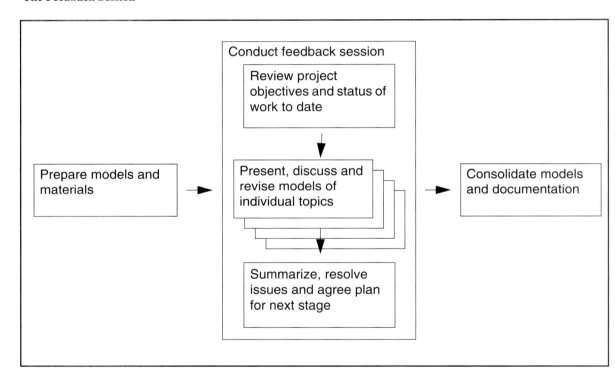

The normal structure for a feedback session is to break the scope into individual topics which are then presented and discussed in turn. For example, in the Guest Administration System, the topics might have been Guest Registration, Regular Guest Programs and Accommodation Administration. The session closes with a discussion which summarizes the overall scope and deals with any outstanding issues or incompatibilities between the individual topics. Each presentation is of a part of the models, primarily the information and function models, and is illustrated by examples of what is implied by the models and counter-examples to illustrate what is excluded by accepting the models. The users have the right to demand any changes they want to the models, the consequences of which can then be examined until the models are a true representation of the balanced view of the experts.

Specific Fast-track Techniques

Fast-track techniques are primarily concerned with increasing user involvement in the project and increasing the speed with which user contributions can be incorporated and fed back. The fast-track techniques rely on good interpersonal skills, but also introduce new ways of working.

Workshops for Scoping

The objective of a scoping workshop is to deliver a clear and prioritized list of the business functions that the proposed system is to support. At the time of the workshop it may not be possible to know exactly what is going to be in the committed scope of the project and what may be excluded. By prioritizing the scope, we provide guidance for including and excluding particular facilities when planning, estimating and resourcing the project.

Priorities set in scoping workshops should represent the value, or expected benefit, of computer support for a particular business activity. Project planning will estimate the cost. Just because a particular activity is perceived to be of higher priority does not mean that support for it will be included in the system before support for any lower priority activities. If it is more expensive to support the first priority than the second, third and fourth together, the project may exclude the first because there is insufficient time or resources to do all four, and the combined value of the second, third and fourth activities exceeds that of the first. When such an opportunity to juggle priorities arises, there always needs to be some debate about cost to the development and benefit to the user. If we could ascribe a quantitative value to computer support for each activity, the cost-benefit equation could be calculated mechanistically. In reality there is a subjective element. The use of priorities helps us to identify such opportunities, but the sponsoring user is the final arbiter on whether this or that facility or group of facilities has more value.

The workshop process is described in great detail in Billings and Billings (1993).

Workshop Deliverables

The scope will be described in terms of a business function model and a single top-level dataflow diagram or context diagram. Where possible, an initial entity relationship model should be produced and cross-referenced to the function model. The entity model is not essential for defining the scope, which, from the user point of view, should focus on the business functions or activities to be supported. Any information that can be gathered about the information used by these functions will save effort later. At this level a dataflow model and a function decomposition are interchangeable; the choice should depend on the preferences of the users and the skill sets of the development team. As a guideline, dataflow models or dependency models are good for tracing a multi-step business process through from start to finish. Function decomposition is better for identifying all the processes and process steps that need to be carried out.

Example:

Guest Administration Scope

In the scoping workshop for the Guest Registration system the analysts used a dataflow model to show the process of check-in (Figure 3-14); for corporate account requirements they used function decomposition (Figure 3-15).

Figure 3-14
The Guest Check-in Process

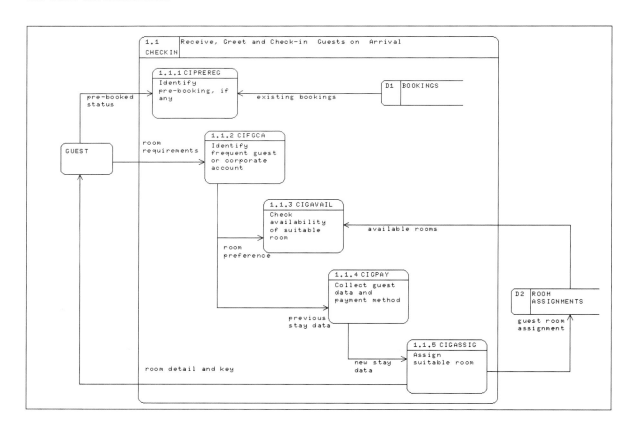

Figure 3-15
Processing Corporate Accounts

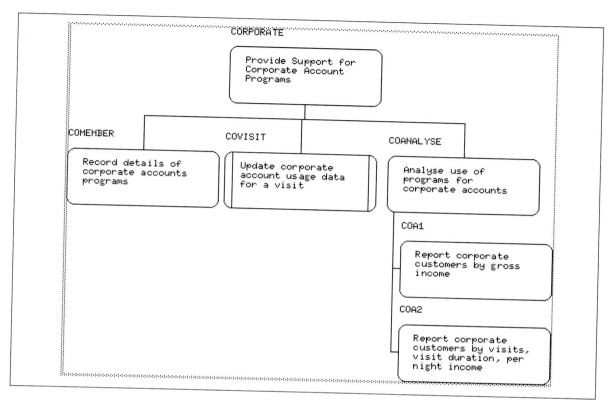

Conducting the Workshop

We could conduct a scoping workshop by inviting the sponsors along, sitting them in front of a blank whiteboard and CASE tool screen and just asking, "What would you like the system to do?". This might work, but it is likely to lead to lengthy unstructured discussions and debate.

In order to complete the scoping exercise as quickly as possible, it is better to provide some initial structure. There are a number of ways the development team can do this.

- A Synthesized Model: they could create a model based on their knowledge of the business area, or they could be given a briefing from the sponsoring user or users and model what they understood from the briefing.

- A Template Model: they could take a template requirements model, prepared by an industry specialist, or a model derived from a previous implementation in the same area of another business.

- An Inherited Model: they could take the appropriate part of the models delivered by an existing information system strategy plan.

- A Prototyped Model: they could refine any of the above types of model by producing prototypes and refining the models based on demonstrations of the prototype to users.

All of these can provide a valid starting point. A particular project should pursue whichever option is the quickest way to achieve the objective of a clear and prioritized list of the business functions that the proposed system is to support. TASK 1, *Scope – by feedback* on page 78, TASK 2, *Scope – by workshop* on page 80 and TASK 3, *Scope – by prototype* on page 82, in the Planning Stage, define how these different approaches fit into the project. Scoping by feedback of an inherited model requires the least preparation time, and fewer controversial issues should arise during the session. Scoping by workshop based on a template or synthesized model is more usual in the many organizations that do not have a formal information strategy plan. Scoping by prototyping is the most time consuming and is discussed more fully below in the section on "Prototyping" on page 61.

Whichever style of workshop is chosen, the conduct is essentially the same. The room should be one in which it is possible to work all day without interruptions. It is best to allow time at the beginning and end of the day for participants to deal with other matters. The practice sometimes used of prearranged breaks during the day is very difficult to control. One person is five minutes late returning, meanwhile another person decides to use that five minutes to make one more call, which then take ten minutes, and so on. Have messages taken and callers intercepted. The facilities in the room should include an overhead projector with blank foils and pens; a whiteboard and pens; plenty of blank paper, including a flipchart, for notes; reference material for any existing systems that are being used as examples; and the CASE tools and capability to project them. The debate about whether or not to use CASE tools during workshops and feedbacks can only be resolved on the basis of efficiency. If the participants prefer to work on paper, foils and whiteboard, and transfer their work to the CASE tools later, then so be it. If everyone is sufficiently relaxed about the use of the tools and their use can save subsequent consolidation time, then they should be used. The CASE tools should never be allowed to get in the way. If they impose a delay whilst the participants works out exactly how to represent what has been agreed, then the tools are not being helpful. Make the notes by some other means and transcribe them later. Real fluency with CASE tools, as with any other medium, comes only with practice. Scoping workshops can provide a great opportunity for that practice, but the first priority is to get the job done, not to show off our expertise and technology.

The Roles of Participants   The roles required for a scoping workshop are sometimes defined as **facilitator, scribe, stakeholder** and **sponsor**. This means that there must be a participant, the facilitator, who is skilled at ensuring that all the subject areas are properly covered, that controversial subjects are given enough, but not too much, time and that all the participants are allowed to contribute to the full extent of their expertise. There must be a participant, the scribe, who is skilled at the modelling techniques that are used (entity relationship, function decomposition, dataflow and dependency) and can transform change requests directly into the corresponding changes to the models. There must also be participants, the stakeholders, who have responsibility for and are knowledgeable about all business areas that are potentially part of the scope. The facilitator and scribe are usually, though not necessarily, members of the development team. The stakeholders are **always** users. They represent the people who will use the system and the people who will receive outputs from the system – the people who have a direct stake in the success of the system. At the scoping stage the stakeholders are often managers responsible for the functional areas within the scope. They are the ones who have a stake in the right scope being set. The sponsor's role is to draw the boundaries around the scope and to arbitrate in any conflict of priority.

It is important to draw the distinction between sponsoring user and stakeholding users. There is a tendency, especially in the informal atmosphere of fast-track projects, to make decisions at the wrong level. Senior managers decide about the layout of screens that they do not have to sit in front of all day. End users make decisions about what should be included in a system they do not have to pay for. Clarifying the roles simplifies the decision-making process.

The facilitator has the responsibility of ensuring that all topics are discussed fully and that the scope of the system support within each area has been agreed and prioritized. The facilitator must also ensure that discussions do not go beyond that level which is helpful. For example, in the Guest Administration System, all aspects of guest registration are equally important and are the first priority. Once we know this, and we have defined what is meant by guest registration by means of a dataflow, dependency or function decomposition model, then there is no value in discussing further detail at this point. If time allows, then such discussion will be helpful and will save time later in a requirements workshop, but it is not strictly necessary to achieve the objectives of the scoping workshop. The facilitator introduces each area, based on the available models (template, inherited, synthesized or prototyped) and leads a discussion that firstly decides scope within that business area and then prioritizes the scoped facilities. Before moving on to the next area the facilitator sums up the decisions reached. After all the areas have been examined in turn the relative priorities of each area, and possibly each facility within the area, will need to be set. This is often the longest session, because it is here that possible conflicts of interest between stakeholders may arise. The facilitator seeks to resolve these conflicts in the workshop if possible, perhaps by means of appeal to the sponsor. If the conflicts cannot be resolved easily, all is not lost. It may be that both requirements can comfortably fit in the scope of the project and hence the dispute is irrelevant. The facilitator's challenge is to balance the need to make progress and the need to control the tendency of the scope to grow ever larger with the need to retain and build the stakeholders' commitment to the project.

The scribe or scribes must translate the comments of stakeholders into more formal documentation. This will eventually take the form of CASE tool models, which will be added to and transformed in the later stages. The scribes must also feed back their understanding, as reflected in the models they are building, to the stakeholders to ensure that there is no misunderstanding.

The stakeholders are there to express their understanding of the business and its needs. Although it is helpful that they understand the process, there should be no need for stakeholders to know any computer jargon or modelling techniques. It is the responsibility of the facilitator and scribes to make sure that the workshop is conducted in language that the stakeholders and sponsor are happy with. Where the stakeholders and sponsor are familiar with the fast-track approach, short cuts can be used.

As system development professionals, we cannot expect business systems users to learn and understand our language in order that they can participate in defining systems built for their benefit and at their cost. We can hardly expect them to commit to a process that feels so alien to them and appears to be run by people with no respect for customer needs.

Prioritizing Requirements

The priorities assigned during the scoping workshop are not ignored after planning is completed. Later in the project, when we may need to re-estimate and replan, the original priorities will provide the rationale for decisions. This places a requirement on the developers to ensure that priorities have not changed. Even when circumstances do not force a replanning exercise, it is worthwhile to review priorities from time to time to ensure that circumstances in the user community have not caused a revaluation of the project, which could then result in revised priorities and a redirected project.

Change is inevitable but conventional wisdom in project management says that the project manager should resist changes to the scope, the so-called scope creep syndrome. One of the most valuable aspects of the fast-track approach is in providing a more responsive capability to systems development organizations. If we then limit that responsiveness, we limit the value of the approach. By using scoping workshops and prioritizing the activities to be supported by the system, we provide a mechanism for costing the response to any change. That cost will not be zero, but at least it can be evaluated against the perceived benefits, and the decision to change or not can be an informed decision, rather than a blanket 'they shall not pass'.

This way of describing and modifying scope relies on a twofold model of priority: the first aspect is the relative value; the second is the decision whether to include it or not, based on a weighting of the value and its estimated cost to implement. The value is subjectively ascribed by the stakeholder; the cost is estimated by the project manager. Both of these can change during the course of the project and lead to reprioritization. The simplest way to express priorities, so that stakeholders, management and developers can see what is expected, is to use the model illustrated in Figure 3-16 below which identifies the different classes of requirements (Must have, Should have, Could have and Won't have – MoSCoW).

**Figure 3-16
Requirements
Priorities and Classes**

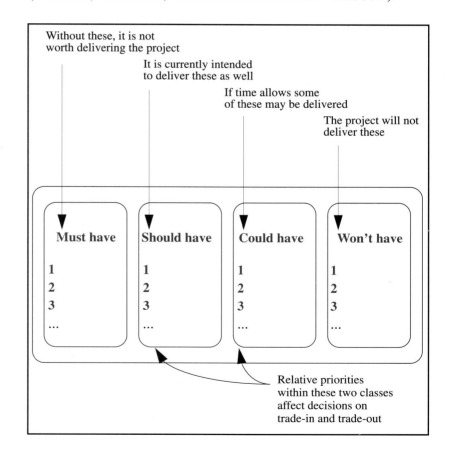

The Oracle CASE tools can easily be extended to define additional properties of each function which represent its priority and classification. Functions can then be displayed and printed through the matrix diagrammer, sequenced and grouped by priority and classification.

Example:
Prioritized Functions

Figure 3-17 below shows how the functions in the Guest Administration System were initially prioritized in the scoping workshop.

These priorities were subsequently revised as a result of the prototyping exercise, not because the list of 'Must haves' is too long but because it was too difficult to deliver this functionality to all the wide variety of potential users.

Figure 3-17
Priorities and Classes
for Guest Administration

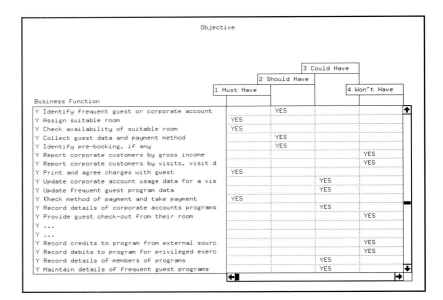

During a scoping workshop it is important to distinguish between the 'Must haves' and the rest, but less important to distinguish between 'Should haves' and 'Could haves'; this latter distinction will become important when we have some estimation of the cost, and will become critical if we are using a timebox implementation. The 'Won't haves' are worth documenting because they represent a clear indication of what is beyond the scope of the current project, which may save time in fruitless debate later. They can also provide an initial candidate list for a later project, because they typically represent issues which the stakeholders have raised, but which are either too expensive (and possibly technologically difficult) to do in the project or else are in a different (but probably related) area of the business which is definitely beyond the current scope. Within the 'Must have' category, priorities are not relevant – they will all be included. Likewise in the 'Won't have' category, they will all be excluded. Within

'Should have' and 'Could have' categories, the priorities, weighted by cost estimates, will be used to make decisions on what will be traded out (from should to could) if time is slipping, and what will be traded in (from could to should) if time becomes available.

Workshops for Requirements

The objective of a requirements workshop is to provide a development team with a clear definition of what a system must do, within the scope defined for the workshop, usually a whole fast-track project or an agreed partition of such a project. What a requirements definition consists of and how it is to be documented is not radically different from the contents and form of the same deliverable produced in the course of a more traditional project. The difference lies in the means by which it is produced, and the greater speed at which it can be produced.

The principle of the requirements workshop is that the definition is arrived at in an open forum of stakeholders and developers, working together. Anyone who has taken part in any such meeting will know that such forums have to be carefully managed if they are to reach a conclusion in a reasonable time. A requirements workshop is more complex than a scoping workshop because usually the number of participants is greater and there must be more attention to detail, which introduce more opportunities for controversy. Conducting all the user interviews at the same time and being able to discuss any issues or contradictions that arise immediately means that the elapsed time to complete the specification of requirements is much shorter, provided the workshop does not descend into an unproductive talking shop! And that is the challenge of workshops – to make sure they work. To achieve this we must define the format of the session, define the roles for the participants, and make sure that we stick to them in practice.

Conducting the Workshop

In the section on "Workshops for Scoping" on page 49, we discussed the roles of participants. Much of this is common to requirements workshops, the critical difference being one of detail. In a requirements workshop we are trying to get enough detail of a business function to actually build computer support for it. The models are the same – entity relationship and function, but the levels of detail which must be included are greater than is necessary for setting the scope and the architecture model, expressing the structure of the system, will start to emerge. This means that the workshop covers the ground more slowly than a scoping workshop: each of the activities identified in the scope has to be explored further, to identify what elementary business functions are involved. For each elementary function we need to establish what information it uses, when it is performed, what business rules apply, and what is the context for the rules – are they invariant, are they specific to this particular activity or are they dependent on a particular user or type of user performing the activity? By using this function-driven approach to detailed specification we are matching the way the users think of their jobs. When we do so, however, we must be careful to ask the qualifying questions concerning the information used and created, and the events that are being responded to and triggered.

Participants and Roles

The roles and skills of facilitator and scribe are very much the same as in a scoping workshop but the role of stakeholder is somewhat different and the sponsor will not necessarily be present. In a scoping workshop the stakeholders are likely to be user managers. In a requirements workshop, the stakeholders may well include some of the same people, but should also include end users. End users are stakeholders: if they feel involved in the process, right from specifying the requirements, they will have a vested interest in the success of the system. If, however, they do not feel that the system is built to meet their needs, their acceptance will be reluctant and less complete. These people should be selected on the basis of their knowledge of the day-to-day conduct of the job, to balance their managers' knowledge of the overall objectives. But they should also be people who have the respect of the rest of the end users, people whose endorsement of the system will lead to general acceptance.

Modelling in Workshops

Before we can be assured that we have the complete requirements models we need to have functions (or business activities), information and events and key results documented, and we must also understand how these all relate to each other. The information model will act as a source for the database design, which will be essential if we are to reuse and share the information with other users and other systems. The events and key results provide us with the checklist for the objectives of the system, so that we can be sure that the scope of the system can be related back to the objectives of the business. For example, the Guest Registration System has to be able to respond to a walk-in booking, a phone booking, a group booking and maybe several other events. Whether or not these are dealt with by the same mechanism is not as important as the fact that if the system does not cope with them all it has not met its objectives. The function model identifies the activities that people carry out to respond to an event or to create the desired results. For example, another objective of the Guest Administration System may be to produce utilization statistics for hotel management. By linking this key result back to the functions that create it and to the information that they use, and to the functions that capture that information, we can be sure that the system definition is consistent and meets its objectives.

Example:
Achieving a Key Result

In the Guest Registration System, senior management requested that room utilization statistics be made available. The dataflow diagram in Figure 3-18, created from information gathered at a requirements workshop, shows that if the key result of utilization statistics is to be achieved, then all the functions in the chain which create the information needed become mandatory.

Figure 3-18
Function Dependency Chain

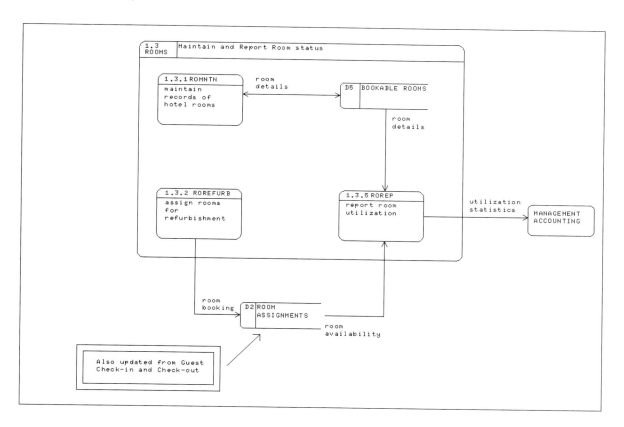

Chains like the one illustrated in Figure 3-18 above are very useful in indicating the interdependency of functions and sometimes will have impact on previous scoping decisions. We may realize that a previously low priority function becomes high priority because it provides a key piece of information for another high-priority function. This can be unfortunate, but we must accept this risk or model the scope in great detail. More commonly, the high-level models created at scoping are subsequently refined but not invalidated and, on balance, it costs less to fix the changes to scope at the requirements stage than it would cost to model the scope at a sufficient level of detail to eliminate the risk.

The Function Model

Users are at their most comfortable talking about their jobs in terms of the activity or activities that they carry out. After all what does the word 'job' mean? It means the things we do, not the information we process or the events we respond to or the results we seek to achieve. Although we need to know about all of these to define a job fully and accurately, the fact remains that, informally at least, people talk about what they **do**.

This means that the function model is the best place to start if you want to work informally with people who do not necessarily have the skills and experiences of computer systems development professionals and who do not need those skills. A workshop is meant to cut through barriers, allowing people to work together productively and informally. The facilitator should start from the function model created at scoping time and discuss each function area in turn with the objective of defining the function down to the elementary business function level. By elementary business function we mean one which if started, must be completed successfully, or if it fails, any changes made up to the point of failure must be undone. For example, in the Guest Administration System a guest arriving at the front desk to check in triggers an elementary business function: either we find them a room or we do not. Although there are a number of steps to the check-in, all of these must complete satisfactorily or the whole process fails.

Elementary business functions form the basis for defining the facilities that the system will provide. The link between functions and facilities is not necessarily one to one but, for any elementary business function that is within our scope, we should be able to point to at least one facility that supports it. For an elementary business function requirement to be completely documented, we need to know who performs it (business units), what data it uses (entities, attributes and relationships) and how it uses it (create, retrieve, update, delete), when it is performed (triggers and events, frequency) and under what constraints (context-specific validation, special processing).

The Information Model

The information model, in the form of an entity model, represents all the entities, relationships, attributes and unique identifiers used by all the elementary functions in the scope of the project. Before the completion of requirements, the entity model is transformed into a relational database design – see the section on "Default Database Design" in *Oracle CASE Dictionary Reference Manual* (Oracle Corporation 1994a) – and additional constraints specified for tables and columns, for example to specify validation of one column dependent on another. Some of these constraints will come up in the workshops and should be documented there and then; others will not emerge until the stakeholders have reviewed the design prototype; some others will not emerge until later still. But that is the real world: we need to acknowledge the facts and work with them, not try to deny them.

Prototyping

Prototyping and iterative development have very different objectives at different stages of the project, and what happens to their deliverables is also very different, although they use very similar tools and techniques. What characterizes a prototype is that it may be discarded when it has been completed. A prototype illustrates what is intended. It is not necessarily part of the eventual deliverable of the development process.

Prototyping and iterative development make extensive use of generator technology. In an Oracle CASE environment, the facility to reuse and share a set of database definitions and sets of user interface design rules or style guides, available as generator preferences and template forms, means that prototypes can be created very quickly. If the prototype is not satisfactory, it may be discarded, the underlying rules and definitions modified, and the prototype generated again. The deliverables are the underlying definitions of functional scope, database design and style guide, not the prototype itself, which is only interesting because it provides an easily accessible example of those definitions and rules.

Requirements Prototype

It may not be possible to set the scope of a project by feeding back to the sponsor an existing outline requirements model, or by synthesizing such a model in a workshop. It may be necessary to evolve the model together with sponsors and stakeholders. This can be done by creating a prototype, perhaps of only part of the possible scope initially, and demonstrating it widely. We may use such a requirements prototype to present to the users what is known to date as a means of checking that it is right, but more importantly at this stage to find out what is wrong and/or what is missing. A requirements prototype takes more time and effort than a workshop or feedback session, but it may be the only way to proceed if there is no one person or small group of people who can define the scope.

Example:

Guest Administration Requirements Prototype

In Chapter 1, we looked at how the Guest Administration team used a requirements prototype to check their understanding with a wide group of users. They quickly built a prototype and demonstrated it at the staff training centre to a wide-ranging cross-section of the user community. They needed to do this because they were not sure exactly what was required. In fact, what happened as a result of that exercise was that the scope of the project was altered. The same functionality was required, but it was only to satisfy the needs of a smaller group of users, who had a greater commonality in their needs.

This is typical of a requirements prototype; it is a mechanism to illustrate the current understanding of the development team and to request a decision on how to proceed. The outcome in our example was to limit the user base.

It may equally be to limit the functionality or even to expand the functionality. In this last case the project would need to be replanned to accommodate the increased scope. This is sometimes not an outcome to be welcomed, but if the project as originally scoped does not satisfy a user need adequately, then it is better to know about it now, when only a small proportion of the investment has been made, than later when the costs have accumulated.

Convergent and Divergent Prototypes

This example shows that there are two different kinds of requirements prototypes, the convergent prototype, where a wide requirement needs to be focused to scope a manageable project, and the divergent prototype where one or more areas of the business first need to be explored, expanding the scope, to identify the best opportunities. A convergent prototype will usually form the basis of a project immediately. The requirements identified will be well documented and can be used to drive that development.

Much of the scope covered by the divergent prototype may not be developed further in the short term and so a fully documented prototype would be unnecessary. This leads to a different approach to tool support in the two types of prototype. Convergent prototypes will normally be CASE tool based, because of the productivity benefits gained from reuse of the repository-based definitions during the rest of the project and beyond. Divergent prototypes may be built using fourth-generation programming languages (4GLs) such as Oracle Forms, because many of them will be discarded or implemented as short-term instant solutions (see "One-shot Fast-track" on page 170). Figure 3-19 opposite illustrates the use of the two types of requirements prototypes.

Look and Feel Prototype

When reviewing a prototype, users frequently comment on the appearance and behaviour, the 'look and feel' of the user interface to the prototype. If this is a pilot project, or the first project for a particular group of users, it will be necessary to identify what style of interface is most acceptable to the users and is consistent with existing user interface standards. This could be done as part of the design prototype, but it can be done more efficiently at an earlier stage. The look and feel can be prototyped by trying various screen designs and report layouts and reviewing them with the users to ascertain what the interface style should be. This can then be documented as a set of rules or a style guide for reuse first in the design prototype, and later in the build stage. A common style guide will save time and will improve the consistency of the user interface.

Design Prototype

A requirements prototype is not a necessary deliverable; it will be produced if it is needed to answer specific questions about the project scope or direction. If there is no ambiguity or problem, a requirements prototype will not be needed. A look and feel prototype will only be necessary if there are

Figure 3-19
Convergent and Divergent Prototypes

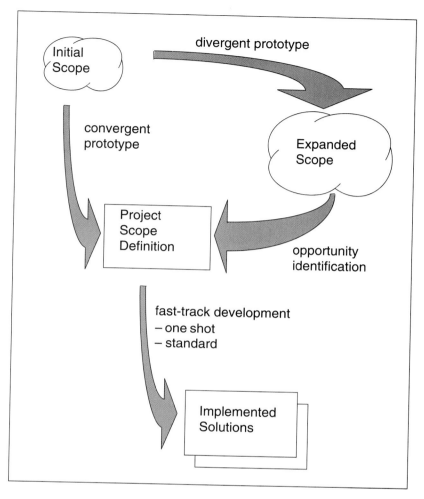

no existing standards for user interface design, or if the standards must be updated for a particular project, perhaps because it is using new technology. All fast-track projects will, however, produce a design prototype, because the design prototype has a very different objective. The design prototype is created from the completed requirements definitions together with the style guide that may have been evolved from the look and feel prototype.

The design prototype is the critical deliverable for the requirements stage. Some practitioners put design prototyping into an entirely separate stage of its own; others regard the first task of the build stage as the construction of the design prototype. The design prototype is important because, as with any prototype, the user can see more clearly what is implied by the documentation if it has been transformed into a working prototype. The best way to test that the requirements have been defined as the user expects is to show them to the user. The design prototype effectively says to the user, *"This is the system we think you asked for. Now tell us what's wrong with it."*

In the usual case some parts of the design prototype will be acceptable and need no further work, except perhaps the addition of user help. The design prototype is usually retained; it is used to incrementally evolve the final system. The requirements prototype and look and feel prototype, are rarely retained after they have served their purpose in clarifying the scope of the project and the rules for user interface design.

Iterative Development

The objective of iterative development is to produce an acceptable deliverable that can be implemented for production use, unlike the products of prototyping which are often discarded. That is why we make a distinction in the terminology between iterative development and prototyping, even though the techniques and tools used are similar.

Where we are working with more than one partition in the development of a project, the impact of changes requested can cross boundaries. A change requested by one user may affect a facility being developed for another user; for example, the validation applied to or the appearance of a data item shared between the two users. We try to choose partitions to minimize the risk of external changes (see "Partitioning the Project" on page 21) but we can never guarantee that changes requested will not cross partition boundaries.

So we must plan accordingly. Figure 3-20 opposite indicates the need to analyse the impact of cross-partition changes and implement them during the iterations. To do this we have to synchronize the development of all the partitions: they should all reach user review at the same time. This can cause problems where a delay in one partition can threaten to delay the whole project. There are two aspects of the response to this threat, one proactive, one reactive. Proactively, partition scoping should take into account the relative speed of the assigned developers and any difficulties such as access to users for review which are likely to cause a particular partition to progress more slowly than the rest of the project. Reactively, it may be necessary to exclude one delayed partition for a cycle and integrate it next time round. This will increase the overall risk to a degree but will avoid delay. If this approach is necessary, then it should still be possible to report changes with cross-partition impacts, even though the resolution of any clashes may be delayed. Once again the balance is between risk and progress, and once again our attitude to risk is to know it and manage it, rather than avoid it.

Figure 3-20
The Iterative Development Life-cycle

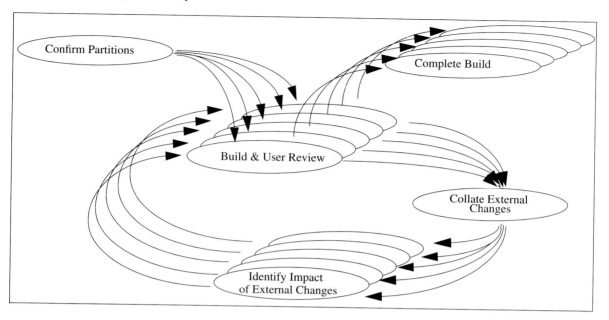

In reality there is an another tactic that we can employ, which is to keep the team informed of cross-partition impacts. In a large formal project such a mechanism would not be effective and the only safe way to manage would be by collating the changes and their impact on other partitions at a synchronization checkpoint; but in a fast-track project of perhaps four to six experienced developers, it is viable for each developer to take responsibility for communicating any change that she or he is requested to make to any other developers that may be affected. Frequently it is only one or two other team members who are affected, and they can assess the impact informally and implement the necessary changes in their current build iteration without waiting for the next synchronization. This approach confers three benefits: firstly, the dependency on synchronization is decreased, and the risk associated with one or more developers missing a cycle is lessened; secondly, the whole process can be short-circuited and changes appear and are dealt with sooner with less delay and effort; and thirdly, the cross-partition synchronizations will be conducted more quickly and easily because most changes will have been already dealt with and implemented. It is still probably worth keeping this as a separate task, just as a way of making sure that no impact has been missed by the more informal approach.

Prototype and Build
Iteration Reviews

Getting User Feedback

The objective of a prototype review or a build iteration review is not to show off how quickly we can develop smart software. It is to find out what is wrong with the smart software we have developed (which isn't nearly so much fun). This is an important attitudinal factor. We all like to be praised for our work, and reviews seem to offer an excellent opportunity, but that is not how the stakeholders see it. A review is their opportunity to make sure that what they are being offered is what they want and need, and there are bound to be some aspects that need to be changed.

The challenge of the review process is to understand what the change is that is being requested and, more importantly, what the change is intended to achieve. What is to be achieved is all-important because there may be a better way, which can then be suggested to the user. Better, in this context, means simpler to implement, more flexible in the event of later change, with less impact on other parts of the system or more consistent with the rest of the system. Even if there does appear to be a better solution to the problem, the stakeholder may prefer his or her original request. How such dilemmas are resolved is an important measure of success for the prototype review process. It is a delicate balance between development cost and end-user benefit. A clear definition of the project scope and timescales is vital here. If the change can be made without affecting agreed costs and time, we have a win-win situation. If the change imperils the project plan, it could be a matter for review by the sponsor. To avoid frequent arbitration meetings for small details, it is important for all participants to buy in to the principle that speed is of the essence. Any significant changes go onto the 'Could have' list and get reviewed at the planned time. It may be necessary to violate this policy, but only rarely.

Preparing for the Review

There should be less need to prepare materials for a prototype/build iteration review, because the system itself is the object of review. However, it is advisable to prepare documentation, including an agenda:

1. Current priorities of all requirements.

2. All the modules that need to be reviewed (including menus).

3. All changes raised which were implemented during the last review.

4. All change requests still outstanding at the last review which have been implemented.

5. All change requests outstanding from the last review which have not been implemented.

6. Any other issues that have arisen in the development; for example, implementation of one of the previous review's outstanding changes in a way which was different from that discussed.

7. Plan of work to next review.

8. Agenda, including:
    i. review of modules changed from last review
    ii. review of issues raised since last review
    iii. review of modules developed since last review
    iv. review of priorities with respect to outstanding work
    v. review of plan of work and risks
    vi. any other issues.

Much of this documentation will exist already, but have it organized and to hand to help the review to go smoothly.

There need only be two people, a developer and a stakeholder, at a review. The project manager may feel the need to be present to support a junior developer, but he or she should not find it necessary to attend all reviews. Sometimes more than one stakeholder will be present. This may be necessary if more than one group of users is to be represented. It may also be preferred if there is no single authority in the user population. However, one-on-one is the most productive, provided both are confident and experienced in their roles. Only have more people if absolutely necessary.

A review should take no more than half a day. Most people find it difficult to work in this way for longer periods of time. In general, if the review cannot be completed in half a day, then the scope is probably too great and it would be better divided into two sessions.

The conduct of the review does not have to follow rigidly the example agenda suggested here, but all the points will need covering. Points i to iii will need to cross-reference the prepared documentation to be sure that nothing gets missed (see also "Test Planning and Testing" on page 33). The reason for emphasizing prepared lists and agenda is as a means of managing time. It is very easy to spend a disproportionate amount of time on one module and then be short of time for the rest. Work out how much time is available to each step and try to stick to it. If it turns out to be inadequate, take a break, rescope the session, plan the next one, and then carry on. Use a visible clock to remind yourselves of the time and if you find your estimates are consistently wrong for the project and the users you are working with, then make sure this gets fed back into the project planning activities.

A Word of Warning

Many of us suffer from two great temptations in user reviews. Firstly we have a nearly uncontrollable urge to justify everything about the work we have prepared for review. Secondly, we conveniently ignore signs that stakeholders are satisfied **only** because they have not understood all the implications of the system as they have seen it. The first of these failings is a combination of ego and laziness; nobody likes to have their errors pointed out, especially if they have to correct them. The second is pure laziness. They are both human failings and many systems developers seem to suffer from them. They must be resisted, and unfortunately no amount of experience and no elegant fast-track techniques can eradicate them. But to be forewarned is to be forearmed, and the review process can be organized to minimize them.

Conducting the Review

Just as in preparing the agenda for a review, there is no necessity to follow a specific rigid form; all developers eventually evolve a style that suits them. But even if you have a preferred format for a review, be prepared to adjust it to accommodate the stakeholder. The list below indicates the general form that all reviews will take.

Take each of the system facilities to be reviewed:

1. Briefly recap what the purpose is, and how it fits into the rest of the system. Demonstrate how the facility is invoked if possible.

2. Use the facility to work through an example of the business function it is there to support. Use realistic data and, at this stage, use correct data. Have the stakeholder operate the system, if he or she feels comfortable with it. If the facility has been reviewed before, just show any changes requested that have altered the behaviour of the facility since the previous review. Make sure that any unusual or complex aspects of the facility are fully covered.

3. Retest the facility to illustrate:

   i. business exception processing; not for all the data value tests or logic tests that are part of unit testing, but for those that represent exceptional processing from the user's point of view. A good example might be to show how check-in proceeds if the expected preregistration is not in the system. A less helpful example would be to show what happens if the room number assigned is invalid; we expect simple invalid data to be handled correctly in a standard way.

   ii. non-standard look and feel; for example, if error handling or help facilities are required to be different.

4. Summarize how the implementation matches the original requirement and any changes requested in previous reviews.

5. Identify any changes still outstanding (and why).

6. Summarize the changes requested during the review. If these contradict a change previously requested, double-check that this is what is required, and make a note. This can happen quite legitimately if the original change request was along the lines of *"What would it look like if..."*, but too many of these can consume a significant amount of time and indicate a tendency to flip-flop between different but equally valid ideas.

Once again, this is not really meant as a strict order of steps, more as a checklist of objectives to have been achieved by the end of the review. This process must be comfortable to both developer and user. Sometimes a formal agenda helps, by providing structure and predictability. Sometimes it obstructs the flow of a more interactive review. Only experience can hone an individual's style, but guidelines can make it possible to start the process of gaining that experience.

Reviewing Priorities

Priorities may need to be reviewed because the project is slipping behind schedule or running ahead of schedule or because the sponsor identifies a change of priority, perhaps triggered by reviewing a development iteration. Priority review is a two-stage process. Firstly the sponsor reappraises the classes and priorities of the current scope, then the project manager assesses the cost of any proposed changes. If there is an available estimate (this need only be a relative estimate in the first instance), the sponsor and project manager can assess the relative degree of impact and make decisions at the time of the initial review. Normally the project manager needs to assess the impact and make a proposal. For example, it is often true that the cost of implementing a particular facility at the same time as another is less than the cost of adding it in later. Likewise, the saving from excluding a facility that could be implemented with another related facility is less than it will cost to include it later. Even with good tool support, this sort of fine-tuned impact analysis can take time. The objective of the Must have/Should have/Could have/Won't have model is to reach most scoping decisions swiftly, on the basis of relative cost and benefit, without the need to produce an absolute model for each.

Consolidating Changes

Many of the required changes will have been documented during the review; they may even have been implemented. However, there will be some changes you will not have been able to specify completely during the review itself. These will need to be consolidated afterwards. Changes fall into two classes: those that affect other partitions and those that do not. Generally, the only local changes that are not documented during the review itself are those where it is not clear what is the best way to make the change, or where other sources need to be consulted before the decision can be made. These changes are simple in principle but will take additional time to document. The other class of changes are those which may affect another partition. A typical example would be a change to the database definition; for example, to add a column to a table or change the datatype or size of a column. Another might be to add new validation criteria for a data item. Any other partition that uses the same data will also need to change.

Whenever a request for a change to validation, derivation, appearance or behaviour of a data item arises, you need to immediately qualify it with the question, "*Is that always true, whenever this data is used, or is it only true in this particular module?*" You are really asking whether the change is global, and could affect other partitions, or whether it is local, with no external impact.

If the project includes more than one partition, the design prototypes of each should be reviewed together if possible. If we synchronize the reviews, the impact analysis and cross-partition changes can be handled at a single session of the whole team. If there are more than two partitions there may be changes that do not affect all the partitions and so some of the team may be wasting time in a consolidation session for the whole team. In practice this is not usually an issue, and the consolidation sessions, both at design prototype time and during build iteration, can serve an additional purpose of bringing the team together to make sure everyone is aware of what everyone else is doing.

Assessing Impact on the Plan

The estimates of required changes may be relative but if the scope creeps the cost estimates should reflect this. If the number and complexity of interdependencies between partitions increase, then the risk profile of the project may alter. The impact on the project of both scope changes and risk changes needs to be assessed and the plan altered if appropriate. Frequently the changes are small because trade-ins between the 'Should have' and the 'Could have' list balance, but even so it is worthwhile to review the plan briefly after prototype and build iteration reviews. If two or more reviews take place at the end of the cycle then the plan review follows consolidation of changes.

Stub Modules for Non-Prototyped Functionality

It may not be possible to generate some modules of the system directly from analysis definitions and hence producing a prototype may be relatively expensive. At the time of the design prototype though, it may be desirable to show how these parts of the system are integrated. If possible avoid prototyping modules that have no direct user interface, such as background updating runs, but, if it is necessary to do so, then the best way is by generating a 'stub module', which is invoked in place of the real module, and which provides documentary commentary on the proposed functionality to be available at that point. A stub module performs no function other than perhaps to display a message that it has been invoked. It is used to represent a module yet to be developed. Stub modules are useful in user reviews to indicate the point at which a particular facility would be invoked and for completeness.

Creating a stub module is a simple process in Oracle CASE:

1. Create a module of type Screen named STUBxxx where xxx is the name of the real module it represents.

2. Provide module-level Help to summarize the specification of the represented module.

3. Link the stub into the system architecture, by means of the module network, at the point where the real module will be linked in eventually. The real module will be stand-alone at this stage and not linked in.

4. Generate the stub based on a template form called STUB, which should have been set up to contain boilerplate information to the effect that the module is a stub.

5. Define one read-only table usage of the main table used by the real module (this is necessary to generate the screen).

Eventually, the real module will be developed and will replace the stub in the system architecture. The stub can then be deleted. At review time, any changes requested to the module represented by the stub should be documented as part of the definition of the real module to be implemented, not the stub.

Summary

Fast-track is about creating small teams of developers and users, teams that can work together and understand the business need to be satisfied, the technology to be used and the time pressure on them. The team members will need good interpersonal skills as well as the professional skills and knowledge they bring to bear. They will need to maintain a sense of urgency and temper that with the pressures of working in small groups.

The techniques of fast-track blend rigorous modelling approaches with more informal workshops. The approach relies on the automation of CASE tools and centres around the 'show me' principle. Prototypes are created, evolved, and if necessary, discarded in a rapid, but ordered progress towards a delivered system.

Chapter

4

PLANNING STAGE

Overview

In this chapter we will look at the process of creating a viable project plan for a fast-track project. To create a plan for the full life-cycle, from requirements to integration, the project manager needs some information about the project, including scope, scale and complexity. If these are not available, for example, from a strategic information systems plan, an initial scoping study will be needed before the plan can be completed. Figure 4-1 below shows how planning and scoping are interrelated.

Figure 4-1

Planning in the

Fast-track Life-cycle

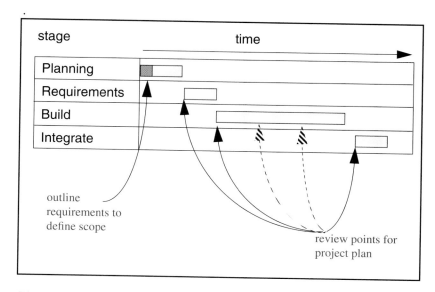

The process of developing the plan has a great deal in common with project planning in any environment. The major difference for fast-track projects lies in partitioning the project and in identifying the right approach to each partition, iterative and/or timeboxed, and so in this chapter we will concentrate on those aspects of project planning, and leave a more general treatment to others (for example Reiss, 1992). Even after it is complete, the plan should be reviewed at the start of each stage and within the build stage additional plan reviews should be scheduled. These would normally be after user reviews in iterative build, and at milestones in timeboxed formal build. The plan reviews should revisit the assigned priorities in the light of the remaining available time and effort.

Objectives

The reason for planning is to make it easier to complete the subsequent project successfully. The plan should be there to help. Since the primary objective is speed, the planning process should not take a long time and the plan must not impose a heavy administrative load.

The objective is to produce a plan which has:

- simplicity
- clarity
- consistency.

Avoid planning and monitoring processes that involve multiple sign-off authorities and multiple reviews. Identify single points of authority, perhaps one per partition for a multi-partition project. Avoid plans that require the team members to provide detailed or complex reporting of their activities. Trade-off control for trust. Fast-track team members will be skilled and motivated: treat them accordingly. Be sure that there are clear quality goals for all deliverables. It is not enough to define what the team must do; the plan should define how we will know when we have succeeded. This is the quality plan and it should enable the team to understand what is expected. The quality plan may not call for inspection of the test scenarios but only for sign-off of the test results from the stakeholder. If that is what is expected, then make it clear.

Major Deliverables

The major deliverables should make it possible to proceed to the next stage. They are:

- a clear definition of the project scope
- prioritization of the scope
- the plan for the project.

A Clear Definition of the Project Scope	The scope may be defined by a combination of workshops, feedbacks and prototypes. But however it is arrived at the definition must clearly identify what the project is expected to deliver. The format will normally be some level of function decomposition model or dataflow model indicating the processes to be supported. The scope should also identify the different partitions of the development and which stakeholders are authorized to agree successful completion for each.

Prioritization of the Scope

Because of the timebox element, the scope must be prioritized and the absolute minimum 'Must have' functionality defined as well as any other 'Should have' features we expect to deliver. It is useful to have a definition of more than we expect to achieve, a prioritized trade-in list of 'Could have' functionality that will be included if time allows. Lastly, a list of 'Won't have' functionality that has definitely been excluded will save fruitless debate later.

The Plan for the Project

Once we have a definition of the scope, we can define the plan in more detail. There are various components of the delivered plan, although they may be merged into one simple document. If so, so much the better, but it is helpful to think of the various components of the plan as a cross-check:

- Resource Plan
  - what resources, people, equipment and facilities will be needed
- Deliverables for the Project
  - what will be produced (for example, system documentation, user help, executable programs)
- Task Plan
  - what activities are required to produce the deliverables
- Quality Plan
  - what measures will be taken to ensure that the deliverables are to the expected quality (for example, quality inspections, regression testing)
- Estimates
  - what effort and elapsed time will be needed for the tasks
- Schedule
  - how the resources are to be deployed to carry out the tasks
- Milestones
  - how we can measure progress during the project.

Critical Success Factors

In planning a project, the essential ingredient is the project manager. His or her skills and knowledge will make or break the project. The project manager must be able to formulate a viable plan and to communicate it to the sponsor and others. To do this he or she must understand the process: the deliverables that are required, the tasks to be done. He or she must have access to the time and attention of the sponsor; if the sponsor and other users do not want the project to succeed, it will fail. Finally, *"the best laid schemes o' mice an' men gang aft a-gley"* (Robert Burns), particularly if there are insufficient or inappropriate resources (people, equipment, facilities, budget) to allow them to succeed.

These critical success factors can be summarized as:

- knowledge of the process

- communication and negotiation skills

- access to and commitment from the sponsor

- availability of suitable and sufficient resources to execute the project.

The Tasks

The major deliverables are, of course, the components of the project plan, but without a detailed statement of the scope we cannot complete the plan. So although the techniques, skills and resources for scoping are essentially those of requirements analysis, we will treat scoping as part of the planning stage. The first task is to set the scope. How this will be done will vary depending on the circumstances of the project. The alternatives are:

- a scoping feedback if the requirement is already defined by a strategy plan

- a scoping workshop if the requirement is not already defined from the output of a strategic planning study

- a scoping prototype if feedback is required from a wide range of sources to identify the boundaries of the project.

Figures 4-2 and 4-3 opposite list the tasks in the planning stage and illustrate the dependencies between them. The tasks are defined in detail in the rest of this chapter.

Figure 4-2
List of Tasks

Sub-stage	Task
Scope Project	Scope – by feedback
	Scope – by workshop
	Scope – by prototype
	Partition the project
	Identify and assign resources
	Complete quality plan
	Complete estimates and schedule
	Review project plan and sign-off

Figure 4-3
The Planning Stage, Tasks and Dependencies

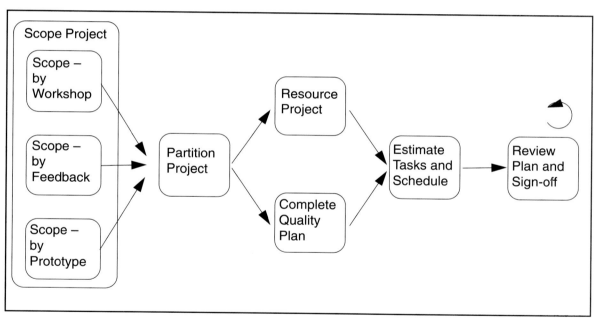

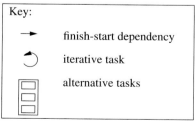

Key:

→   finish-start dependency

↺   iterative task

▣   alternative tasks

Tasks

TASK 1
Scope – by feedback

DESCRIPTION

This task sets the scope of the project by using feedback of part of an existing information systems strategy plan to identify the business functions to be supported.

Steps

1. Review existing documentation (strategy study or other source).

SUB-STAGE
Scope Project

2. Brief participants and identify issues (see notes).
3. Schedule the feedback: room, facilities and participants.
4. Prepare and conduct the feedback.
5. Consolidate results and quality check deliverables.
6. Revise estimates in line with scope and priorities.
7. Identify project risks and recommended risk management strategy.

ESTIMATING: Reviewing existing documentation may be time consuming if team members are not familiar with the source material. The feedback will probably take half a day. Seek to do consolidation during the session if the CASE tool is being used, but allow another day afterwards in case of inconsistencies, and plan for post-feedback contact with the sponsor to resolve any issues.

QUALITY: Use CASE tool consistency checks on the consolidated model. Note that at this stage there may well be incompleteness. We have to leave something for detailed requirements.

NOTES: Briefing the participants can be done in a formal session or by means of short interviews. The latter approach may pre-warn the team of controversial issues that could emerge in the feedback. However, it increases cost and time needed for individual interviews. On balance a group briefing is probably adequate where the requirement is based on a recent strategy plan and the user sponsor is in authority. The scope can be set without necessarily involving all users. Typically the sponsor and one or two other users will be involved. These are not necessarily management; an experienced and respected user can provide a useful counterbalance to a management view.

During the feedback, ensure that the relative priorities of the functions included in the scope are also identified and that any functions which are explicitly excluded are identified as such.

See also "Workshops for Scoping" on page 49, and Tasks 2 and 3 below.

Deliverables

PREREQUISITES

– project objectives

– requirements model
- entity relationship model
- function hierarchy

– identified user sponsor

– budgetary cost estimate

DELIVERABLES

– revised project objectives

– revised requirements model
- function hierarchy
- entity relationship model
- list of business units involved
- entity to function cross-reference (optional)
- business unit to function cross-reference (optional)
- event/function/key result cross-reference (optional)
- dataflow context model (optional)

– prioritized function requirements

– revised budgetary cost estimate

– project risk assessment

TECHNIQUES: The project objectives are expressed as a simple list, possibly prioritized. See "Information Modelling" on page 38.

Requirements modelling is discussed in "Function Modelling" on page 41, "Information Modelling" on page 38 and "Systems Architecture Modelling" on page 44.

The functions are prioritized into four categories (Must have, Should have, Could have, Won't have – the MoSCoW model). These may well be revised during the course of the project. See "Managing Timebox Projects" on page 27.

The information for estimating at this stage is still incomplete, but a top-down estimate based on the list of functions in the scope will be possible. See "Estimating in Fast-track Projects" on page 24.

In any project, and particularly in fast-track projects, it is important for estimating and quality planning to understand the risk factors. "Scoping the Project" on page 19 discusses how to quantify risk in a fast-track project.

TOOLS: The Oracle CASE tools provide facilities to create and revise the requirements models: the Function Hierarchy Diagrammer, Entity Relationship Diagrammer and Matrix Diagrammer. Matrices of event/function/key results can be constructed using user extensibility. Function definitions can be extended to include priority, and the Matrix Diagrammer used to display functions in order of priority.

Tasks

TASK 2
Scope – by workshop

DESCRIPTION

This task sets the scope of the project by using a workshop with the sponsoring user and others to identify the business functions to be supported.

Steps

1. Brief project sponsor and select appropriate approach.

2. Brief other participants and identify issues (see notes).

SUB-STAGE
Scope Project

3. Schedule the workshop: room, facilities and participants.

4. Prepare and conduct the workshop.

5. Consolidate results and quality check deliverables.

6. Revise estimates in line with scope and priorities.

7. Identify project risks and recommended risk management strategy.

ESTIMATING: Allow time for briefing interviews and consolidation (no more than three in a day) and for synthesizing an outline function hierarchy to structure the workshop if necessary (up to one day). Allow half a day for the scoping workshop itself.

QUALITY: Use CASE tool consistency checks on the consolidated model.

NOTES: At the briefing with the sponsor, you should agree the participants for the workshop. They should have responsibility for and knowledge of all business areas that are potentially part of the scope.

As with scoping by feedback, briefing may be done in a single session or by means of short informal one-on-one interviews. The right approach is probably to have a short (about half an hour) discussion with each participant beforehand to identify the critical issues.

A variant of scoping by workshop is to use a template requirements model of the business area, which may have been created by an industry specialist or may be reused from a previous project. A template may need tuning to match the specific business. If the workshop is based on a template, preparing is equivalent to preparing a feedback. If it is based on just the sponsor's briefing then it will require the synthesis of an outline requirements model.

In clarifying and prioritizing the project objectives a clear mission statement is very useful later when trying to evaluate and re-evaluate the priorities. We can always ask the questions, "*Does it advance the project objectives? Does it support the mission?*"

See Task 1 above and Task 3 below.

Deliverables

PREREQUISITES

– project objectives

– identified user sponsor

– budgetary cost estimate

– template model (optional)

DELIVERABLES

– revised project objectives

– revised requirements model
  - function hierarchy
  - entity relationship model
  - list of business units involved
  - entity to function cross-reference (optional)
  - business unit to function cross-reference (optional)
  - event/function/key result cross-reference (optional)
  - dataflow context model (optional)

– prioritized function requirements

– revised budgetary cost estimate

– project risk assessment

TECHNIQUES: The techniques for a scoping workshop are the same as for Task 1 above.

With no prior model or template, there is an even greater emphasis on the modelling skills of the facilitator and scribe. By getting all the users together in this way and condensing the interview and feedback cycle into a day, we increase the pressure on the project. The team members must be well prepared and confident. If they are not experienced, it may be worth drafting in a more experienced facilitator just for the workshop and consolidation. A good technique for arriving at the project objectives is to challenge large areas of the proposed scope; ask the sponsor, *"If we only did this half of the project, would it be worth doing?", "Or this half?"* In this way we can arrive at a very clear estimate of the relative value of each business area, and can get to the heart of the problem that the system is to solve.

See also "Workshops for Scoping" on page 49.

TOOLS: The tools applicable to a scoping workshop are similar to those used in a feedback. If the workshop is based on a template that includes prototypes already generated, the workshop may also use the Oracle CASE Generators to update these existing prototypes in the workshop so that they reflect changes agreed.

Tasks

TASK 3 *Scope – by prototype*	**DESCRIPTION** This task sets the scope of the project by building a prototype and reviewing it with users to identify the business functions to be supported.

Steps

1. Synthesize requirements model to appropriate level of detail **or**
2. Adapt template model.

SUB-STAGE
Scope Project

3. Adopt look and feel standards.
4. Design prototype database, application and architecture.
5. Generate or build prototype.
6. Populate database with illustrative data for prototype.
7. Review prototype.
8. Consolidate requirements changes and document as necessary.
9. Revise estimates in line with scope and priorities.
10. Identify project risks and recommended risk management strategy.
11. Repeat for further prototypes, revisions or workshops.

ESTIMATING: Scoping by prototype can be the most time consuming way of scoping. A convergent prototype is effectively equivalent in effort to developing a design prototype (see Tasks 6 to 11 in Chapter 5). A divergent prototype can be open-ended and should be timeboxed.

QUALITY: Use CASE tool consistency checks on the consolidated model of a convergent prototype.

NOTES: This approach should be used if there is no single view of the requirements and no clear priorities by which a project could be scoped. Scoping by prototype is often appropriate if a single sponsor cannot be found. A scoping prototype may be used in two ways:

- convergent — Where the identified scope is too wide, a prototype can be used to prioritize requirements to narrow the scope to a manageable project. 'Won't have' features for a project may well be 'Must haves' in a subsequent project.

This is how it was used in the Guest Administration example. What was left out were the variations necessary to support all the different hotels.

- divergent — In a divergent prototype the emphasis is not on identifying which requirements to leave out, but on helping users to see how the technology can best assist them. Such a prototype might identify many requirements which can then be prioritized and possibly phased over more than one project.

If a divergent approach is taken then any number of prototypes may be built, many of which will be discarded. In a convergent approach, the prototype will define some or all of the project scope directly and so will need to be more fully documented. Both will be reviewed by users and possibly revised.

Deliverables

PREREQUISITES

– identified user sponsor

– budgetary cost estimate

– project objectives

– (template model)

– (outline requirements model)

DELIVERABLES

– revised project objectives

– revised requirements model
  - function hierarchy
  - entity relationship model
  - list of business units involved
  - entity to function cross-reference (optional)
  - business unit to function cross-reference (optional)
  - event/function/key result cross-reference (optional)
  - dataflow context model (optional)

– prioritized function requirements

– revised budgetary cost estimate

– project risk assessment

TECHNIQUES: In addition to the use of prototypes, you may also use techniques from Tasks 1 and 2 above.

The construction of protoypes is discussed in "Prototyping" on page 61.

Reviewing prototypes with users to identify changes to the underlying models is discussed in "Prototype and Build Iteration Reviews" on page 66.

See also "Convergent and Divergent Prototypes" on page 62.

TOOLS: A scoping prototype can be developed in the same way as a design prototype, using CASE tools, or it can be created directly in 4GL development tools (for example Oracle Forms). In any one prototype a combination of the two approaches may be used, in which case any of the development tools may be used. The project scope could include some functional objectives that are best met with end-user tools (for example Oracle Data Browser).

A convergent prototype will normally be documented in the CASE repository, consisting of a requirements outline, look and feel preferences, data definitions and module definition. A divergent prototype will normally be defined directly into Oracle Forms or Oracle Reports. These definitions may be reverse engineered into the Oracle CASE tools if the prototype subsequently forms the basis for a development project.

Tasks

TASK 4

Partition the project

DESCRIPTION

This task defines the scope of work packages or partitions that can be developed in parallel.

Steps

1. Identify partitions and stakeholders for each.

2. Identify the iterative and formal build elements.

3. Identify the groupings for requirements workshops.

4. Review and revise risk assessment and estimates.

ESTIMATING: The experienced fast-track manager does this almost intuitively. However, by applying the principles consistently, it should be possible for even a less experienced manager to partition a project with reasonable success in a day.

QUALITY: Applying the cohesion and coupling criteria, you can measure the success of a partitioning. Although it may be possible to improve on a 'first cut', such an exercise will quickly lead to diminishing returns. If multiple re-partitions are used, measure each one against the previous. Is the improvement worth the effort?

NOTES: The objective in partitioning the project is to create work packages that can be developed in parallel. Where interdependencies exist between partitions, then complexity and the possibility of mistakes rise. Hence we want to create partitions that are, to a large extent, independent of each other, for data, for users, and for process.

Whether a partition should be developed by a formal or iterative approach, or a combination of both, is a factor of the degree of user interaction and the degree to which the requirements can be prioritized and traded out.

We may identify several partitions for the development of the system but still decide to conduct a requirements workshop for all of them together. This would be appropriate if the users are the same for all the partitions, or significantly overlap, or if there are dependencies between partitions (if, for instance, they represent different stages of the same business process). Either of these cases indicates that the coupling between the partitions is not optimally low, in which case we might prefer to merge them into a single partition. Even if the coupling is low and the cohesion is high, there are benefits in a single requirements workshop, because then all the participants understand all of the goals of the project. The use of partitions is a convenience for development, and should not be a barrier to user understanding or involvement. If cohesion and coupling are not optimal we may need to revise the project risk assessment.

Deliverables

PREREQUISITES

– requirements model

- entity relationship model
- function hierarchy
- entity to function cross-reference (optional)
- involved business units list
- business unit to function cross-reference (optional)
- event/function/key result cross-reference (optional)

– budgetary cost estimate

– project risk assessment

DELIVERABLES

– requirements workshop definitions

– partition definitions, as subsets of the requirements model

– partitions style definition (formal/iterative)

– stakeholders for partitions

– revised budgetary cost estimate

– revised project risk assessment

TECHNIQUES: In partitioning a project we seek to put together functions that use the same data and functions that are the responsibility of a single business unit. In this way we can minimize dependencies between the partitions and appoint a single user representative (stakeholder) for each partition. "Partitioning the Project" on page 21 discusses this in detail.

TOOLS: Partitioning a project of even modest size is a tedious job without CASE tool support.

By using the Matrix Diagrammer to display matrices of business functions in the scope of the project against the information they use and create (function/entity), we can see where the data dependencies lie, and can group the functions together in order to minimize the interdependency between the groups, which become the candidate partitions. We can also display a matrix of functions against the user groups that perform them (function/business unit) to check where the candidate partitions cross business unit boundaries. Where this happens we can consider moving functions from one partition to another to diminish the people-dependent coupling between partitions.

For some projects, the key objectives are to respond to particular events or to create particular outputs; for example, "*We must make sure that we can immediately find out the state of any room in the hotel and, if it is not available for guest check-in, when we expect it will be*" or "*We must be able to rapidly change the priorities of room maintenance to respond to guest check-in needs*". In cases like this we can use the Dataflow Diagrammer in Oracle CASE Designer to show dependencies chained through business areas to evaluate to what extent each of the business processes identified is to be the responsibility of a single partition. This could be a reason to allow a partition that involves more than one business unit. It might be the best way to achieve the most important objectives of the project.

Tasks

TASK 5
Identify and assign resources

DESCRIPTION

This task identifies the resources necessary to complete the project successfully and ensures that they know what is required of them.

Steps

1. Determine team size.
2. Profile the required skills.
3. Identify and acquire appropriate team members.
4. Allocate work packages.
5. Brief team members.

ESTIMATING: Identifying the resources is easy if you have no choices, but with a large resource pool and conflicting priorities with other projects acquiring the right resources can be a lengthy process. For a particular environment, we should find out how long it normally takes to resource a project. Initially resourcing fast-track projects will be more complex than the team size would suggest, because the required skills may be less widely available.

QUALITY: See below for the major checkpoints. If we cannot tick these off, the resource plan has some potential weaknesses, in which case we need to feed a revision to the project risk assessment into the quality planning activity.

NOTES: When performing the risk assessment at scoping we may not know precisely who the development team members are. When we finalize the team we may need to revise the risk assessment for the factors that are affected by the team. These are:

- availability   Do we have adequate time for each person to do his or her assigned work plus contingency?
- technical skills   Does the team have adequate proven experience in the tools and techniques?
- team skills   Do the team members have a track record for successful working in compact teams?
- fast-track skills   Does the team have experience of fast-track projects, particularly the high level of user participation?
- motivation   Is the team determined to succeed?

The team size is normally a function of the number of partitions but there should be at least one member of the team with experience of each of the fast-track roles as described in "Redefining Systems Development Roles" on page 8.

Deliverables

PREREQUISITES

– budgetary cost estimate

– project risk assessment

– requirements workshop definitions

– partition definitions as subsets of the requirements model

– partitions style definition (formal/iterative)

– knowledge of available resources

DELIVERABLES

– resource plan
  • work package assignments
  • resource availability
  • contingency
  • other commitments

– revised budgetary cost estimate

– revised project risk assessment

TECHNIQUES: Match the available resources to the roles and skills required. There are tools available that allow the user to define a resources or skills database, in which each person can be classified according to what type of resource they are (programmer, project manager, etc.) and what skills they possess and to what level. If such a database is available, then use it. Project managers usually prefer to trust their own judgement and experience or the recommendation of a respected colleague rather than a database, but using a skills database can remind you of the existence of someone you had forgotten or bring to your attention the skills of someone who you did not think was right for the job.

Even if it is available, accurate data is only part of the answer. In a fast-track project, the team members will need to work independently for much of the time (for example, when developing their own separate partitions) and in close cooperation at other times (for example, when resolving the impact that a change in one partition has on the other partitions). They will be under pressure to deliver as quickly as possible and may be using tools and techniques which they have only recently learnt. A good team spirit is vital. The most important technique that a project manager can apply is his or her own leadership.

If interdependencies between partitions are complex, or changes are required to the development team or the appointed stakeholders, then the project risk profile may be affected. Risk assessment is discussed in "Scoping the Project" on page 19.

TOOLS: Some project planning tools provide resource management and skills database facilities and a capability to maintain a database of previous projects as a repository of experience.

TASK 6

Complete quality plan

DESCRIPTION

The quality plan specifies how we are going to measure quality, who will do it and when. The essential task is to identify the right measures, at the right points in the project, and assign responsibility for taking those measures.

Steps

1. Identify variance from standard tasks.

2. Identify high-risk tasks.

3. Define interim deliverables.

4. Define quality milestones.

5. Define quality measures and acceptable values.

6. Define reporting standards.

7. Assign quality roles.

8. Identify contingency activities.

ESTIMATING: Preparing a quality plan for a standard project should take little time; the quality paragraphs on each task definition in this book provide appropriate quality measures. Where the plan varies from the norm difficulties can arise, especially if the quality measure is not apparent.

QUALITY: Even a quality plan must be subject to quality assessment. See the notes below.

NOTES: The critical success factors for a quality plan are:

- completeness

  Do we have a quality measure for each task and deliverable? If necessary, identify interim deliverables which can be assessed. For example, we could use a comparison of the number of changes requested by the user after each review, expecting that this number would decrease each time.

- practicality

  Are all the quality measures quantitative and is the information available in time? For example, it is not a valid quality measure of an interface design that the users find it easy to use. We cannot know that until after implementation. A better measure would be that an appointed representative user, or group of users, had tested it and declared it usable.

In addition to a plan for measuring the quality, we need to know what is acceptable quality and what actions we are going to take if the quality is not acceptable. But the emphasis is on prevention, rather than cure, because prevention is always easier, cheaper and quicker than cure.

Deliverables

PREREQUISITES

– requirements workshop definitions

– partition definitions

– partitions style definition (formal/iterative)

– project risk assessment

DELIVERABLES

– quality plan
  • milestone definitions
        measures
        tools
        acceptable values
        contingency activity
  • partition review points
  • progress reporting standards and mechanisms

TECHNIQUES: There is no point in specifying quality goals that cannot be achieved or measured. Always set measurable goals. Where we have a choice of measure, we may select one or more metrics as representative. The choice will be affected by how easy it is to use each measure, which is where the tools become relevant. A CASE repository that can offer various analyses of its data can provide quality check information very quickly and easily. For example, such questions as, *"Do we have a menu for each type of user?"*, *"Does each menu include options for all the screens and reports that support the functions this type of user performs?"* are easily answered and provide a completeness measure for the application design.

Project management tools provide the most likely mechanism for recording the prerequisites and deliverables of quality planning. If the project management tool incorporates a project templating facility, whereby a project manager can use a previous project plan or a standard methodology plan as the template for the current plan, then quality planning and indeed the whole planning process can be expedited. Experienced project managers rely on and reuse that experience. Less experienced project managers can benefit from the experience of others by consulting the example project plans or the plans and results of actual previous projects.

See "Quality Management in Fast-track Projects" on page 27, "Scoping the Project" on page 19 and "Controlling Formal, Iterative and Timebox Builds" on page 25.

TOOLS: Oracle CASE tools provide quality and completeness reports that provide easily accessible metrics of quality. The Matrix Diagrammer in Oracle CASE Designer provides *ad hoc* cross-referencing which helps identify gaps; for example, a business function for which we do not know the responsible business unit.

Tasks

TASK 7
*Complete estimates
and schedule*

DESCRIPTION
This task confirms the scale of development for each partition and defines the content of the requirements and build stages.

Steps

1. Confirm budgetary estimate for each work package.

2. Adjust estimates for assigned resources if necessary.

3. Add time for quality plan activities.

4. Create project schedule.

ESTIMATING: The effort will go in checking existing data. Provided there is easy access to history and standards, this should not take long.

QUALITY: The quality of estimates can only be judged afterwards, but hindsight for one project is foresight for the next, so creating a project history database will pay dividends in the end. Any estimates should be checked against available history. There may be variance, quite legitimately, but where there is variance from the expected, it should be understood and justifiable.

NOTES: Conventional management wisdom says that the optimum number of people for one person to manage is the magic number seven. On a fast-track project that would almost certainly be too many, because the fast-track manager will be working as a hands-on member of the team as well as managing the process. This is not because the tasks are too difficult for a mere mortal: it is because for some activities 'two heads are better than one'; for example, in interviewing, workshops, feedback sessions, design reviews. Depending on the plan, team members may be able to back each other up for these, and there is an advantage in all the team knowing what others are doing. More flexibility is available to project managers if they schedule themselves without responsibility for development of a particular partition, or at most only a minor one, and make themselves available for backing up the team. This has the additional advantage that the project manager has up-to-date knowledge of all parts of the project.

There is a school of thought which says that adjusting the estimate for specific resources (for example, an expert of guru status) is dangerous because it creates expectations that will not be fulfilled if the key resources need to be reassigned elsewhere. In fast-track projects we should acknowledge the risk, but accept it nonetheless to shorten the planned timescale.

Even where the development is iterative, it is likely that fast-track work packages are timeboxed. As a guideline, the development of a fast-track partition by a single developer from the statement of scope to delivery should ideally take no more than eight weeks. If the requirements workshop is to be shared with other partitions, there will be some people-scheduling constraints that extend the timescales. Likewise if there is limited access to users for reviews the timeline may stretch. Otherwise, if it looks like it will take longer, we should question whether this is best developed as a single partition.

Deliverables

PREREQUISITES

– requirements workshop definitions

– partition definitions

– partitions style definition (formal/iterative)

– quality plan

- milestone definitions
- partition review points
- progress reporting standards and mechanisms

– resource plan

- work package assignments
- resource availability
- contingency
- other commitments

– budgetary cost estimate

DELIVERABLES

– work package estimates

- for requirements stage
- for implementation stage

– task schedule

TECHNIQUES: Estimating, more than any other activity in project management, reuses previous experience. Estimating is a complex and much debated topic in the literature of project management. It is impossible to cite a single definitive text, but Symons (1991) examines function point analysis in detail.

See also "Estimating in Fast-track Projects" on page 24.

TOOLS: Some project planning tools provide automatic scheduling for time and resource constrained schedules and can hold a history of previous projects which can provide estimating metrics. Reports available from Oracle CASE Dictionary can produce a function point count based on the requirements models produced in TASKS 1, 2 and 3.

TASK 8

Review project plan and sign-off

DESCRIPTION

This short task ensures that users, management and team all understand what is intended and that the project plan reflects this intention clearly and accurately.

Steps

1. Review timescales and deliverables with user management.

2. Review resource plan and quality plan with team members.

3. Review timescales (particularly workshops, feedbacks and reviews) with user participants.

4. Revise plan accordingly.

ESTIMATING: For a small project it is best to conduct a single end-of-stage review meeting. If the plan cannot be readily agreed between all parties at this stage, then the risk to the project is very real. This should be a short meeting just to confirm that nothing significant has been overlooked, and that all the players know the part they are to play.

QUALITY: As for all meetings, be sure that the objectives are clear, that attendees are the right people to achieve the objectives and that all the documents and other materials that will be needed by the meeting are available.

NOTES: As well as the plans that indicate what the team will be doing and when, the project plans should include a statement of how progress is to be reported to sponsors and stakeholders. This should include:

- baselines
- milestones
- reporting intervals (weekly, monthly, etc.)
- reporting requirements (e.g. actual versus plan weekly, full analysis monthly)

and possibly

- earned value calculations (value of completed work against cost to date).

These items will frequently have been drafted from a house standard and revised if necessary for the project. See Task 6.

Deliverables

PREREQUISITES

– resource plan

– quality plan

– partition definitions

– cost estimates

– task schedule

DELIVERABLES

– agreed project plan
  • revised resource plan
  • revised quality plan
  • revised task schedule
  • revised progress reporting standards

TECHNIQUES: The management of meetings is part of the general professional skills set that is necessary for any team working. Consistent, good quality presentation of the plans will make it easier for all parties to understand what is expected. Having project management tools available, with what-if analysis capability, can reduce the need for further meetings if revisions are needed because the project manager can make the changes during the meeting and try out alternative plans.

TOOLS: Project planning tools allow the project manager to change project plans to investigate alternatives and either accept the revised plan as the new agreed schedule or reject it and return to the original, perhaps to explore another variant.

Example:

The Guest Administration Plan

In the planning stage of the Guest Registration System project the team built a scoping prototype which they showed to users and user management to try to identify the project boundaries. They had synthesized a suggested model based on their own knowledge of guest administration and after the prototyping exercise put together the plan for the rest of the project. The team and sponsor shared a good understanding of the requirements, but one of the critical aspects of the risk assessment for the project was the wide geographical spread of users and the differing attitudes and experience of their users. As a result of assessing the plan and the risk, the final agreed project was confined to a smaller user population. This reduced the scope, allowed the sponsor and project manager to identify a single stakeholder for each partition and reduced the risk associated with widely distributed users..

Summary

The fundamental objective of the planning stage is for the developers and the sponsor to create and agree a clear picture of what their project will produce, how it will produce it, and how they will monitor its progress. The key word here is **agree**. All the participants, sponsor, user stakeholders, project manager and project team should understand and buy in to the plan, the approach and the required system.

The plans produced should define the minimum set of activities to achieve this objective. Similarly, the plans themselves should represent the minimum set of documentation to support this objective. Be prepared to be creative and flexible, responsive to the uniquenesses of each project in order to maintain the balance of speed and risk.

However, a plan is only of theoretical interest until it is executed. In the next chapter we will see how the requirements emerge and the delivered system begins to take shape.

Chapter

5

REQUIREMENTS STAGE

Overview

In a traditional project, the requirements stage is concerned with **what** the system is required to do rather than **how** it will do it, which is dealt with during the design stage. In a fast-track project we blur this distinction because often the best way to be sure that we have properly understood **what** is needed is to show the users **how** we will satisfy the need and ask for their reaction. Using code generators to produce the design prototype not only provides high productivity, but also ensures that the documented requirements are reflected in the prototype, and changes to the prototype are reflected in the requirements. The two are kept in step because one is simply a transformation of the other. If the design prototype is created by direct use of prototyping tools or 4GL tools, there is still the separate task of documentation, which will probably just not get done.

In a fast-track project the design prototype, also known as a first-cut design, is an essential deliverable. Some practitioners prefer to produce the design prototype in a separate design stage, in order to maintain the **what** versus **how** distinction. From a project deliverables viewpoint this makes little difference. But from a user point of view it is more valid to sign off the design prototype as the specification of the required system, supplemented by notes and descriptions of the necessary additions and changes, rather than a purely documentary definition. For that reason we include production of the design prototype as a requirements stage deliverable and dispense with a separate design stage.

The most logical way to define the tasks required in any stage of a project is to define the deliverables that are required and then to consider the tasks which must be performed in order to create those deliverables. The deliverables themselves are defined in terms of the objectives of the stage.

Objectives

The objectives of the requirements stage are:

- to provide enough information for the rapid construction of the system
- to agree with users what the system is to do
- to achieve this in the minimum time.

The first two objectives appear to conflict with the third, and it is the resolution of this conflict which characterizes the risk management approach of fast-track. Once we understand what is to be achieved, it becomes clearer what deliverables constitute the achievement of these objectives.

During the requirements stage we will also need to be sure that responsibilities for transition needs, data conversion, training and so on have been assigned (See "Transition" on page 165).

Major Deliverables

In order to understand what needs to be done to complete the requirements specification, we need to understand what deliverables are required. We can then identify the appropriate tasks to create these deliverables and select the appropriate tools and techniques to create them as quickly as possible. Because of the evolutionary nature of fast-track projects, the project team will agree with the users **what** is required and then fill in some of the detail of **how** that is to be achieved later. Hence at the requirements stage we only need a sufficiently detailed specification to enable the users to understand what the completed system will do and agree it. The major deliverables of the requirements stage are:

- an information model
- a business function model
- a system architecture model
- a design prototype.

Clearly, the major deliverables from this stage have multiple layers to them. Figure 3-8 on page 40 shows how the information model evolves through the project, until it includes not just the data definitions and the invariants but even defaults for how the data will appear, defaults for help text to accompany the use of the data items, and error messages to be displayed when there is a violation of a rule. Incidentally, you should not assume that later stages will not return to, and revise, levels of the model which were first defined at an earlier stage. You must be able to do so efficiently or else any fast-track benefits will be quickly eroded in rework time. The definitions of tasks in this and subsequent stages show how changes to earlier deliverables are managed.

Information Model

This is normally a detailed entity relationship model, defining entities, attributes, relationships, validation rules and domains for the attributes together with the business rules about data integrity (e.g. referential integrity constraints). These rules, sometimes known as invariants or data invariants, define processing that is associated with data and with specific events applied to data.

Example:

Rules for Guest Administration

We may have a rule that we cannot delete a Frequent Guest record if there are any associated Room Bookings, or another that stipulates that all Room Bookings must be Provisional, Confirmed, Checked-in, Checked-out or Cancelled, and that when we create a new Room Booking the default status is Provisional. These rules are to be applied whenever the appropriate event occurs (e.g. Delete Frequent Guest and Create Room Booking), regardless of who causes the event or what particular module of the system is invoked to process it.

The advantage of recognizing these rules as invariant is that we can specify them once, and reuse them whenever we process this data (Frequent Guest or Room Booking) without having to specify them as part of each module.

This approach of identifying processing rules with the data to which they apply improves productivity (define once, use many times) and quality (consistency is automatically implemented). To realize all the potential benefits of this approach, however, we need to have CASE tools that can structure the information in this way and can automatically include the rules in generated code. Information modelling for fast-track projects using Oracle CASE is described in the section on "Information Modelling" on page 38.

Business Function Model

By migrating much of the data processing into invariants associated with the information model, we reduce the need for detail in the functional model. The requirement of the functional model in fast-track is to identify the facilities that the system must provide, what data they use and for what purposes, and any additional processing rules that are specific to a particular facility. For example, we might define an additional rule for the facility that allows guests to check out using the televisions in their rooms. The rule would stipulate that if the booking does not include a credit card authorization number, then the facility provides a respectful message to the user and exits without completing the check-out. This is not an invariant rule, because if it were a desk check-out, the clerk would request a credit card authorization or another form of payment and then complete the check-out.

System Architecture Model

The system architecture is the blueprint for the design: it represents the skeleton of the system onto which the flesh of the facilities will be built. The section on "Systems Architecture Modelling" on page 44 discusses how the system architecture model is developed through scoping, requirements definition and during the build stage. Much of the detail is added later, but the definitions of which business units are responsible for which elementary business functions is the starting point that should be captured in the requirements workshop. The development of the design prototype is then made easier.

Design Prototype

The design prototype contains no more than is already recorded in the information model, the function model and the architecture model. However, because it is a working system, it is much more useful than just the documentation when agreeing with the sponsor and stakeholders what the system is to look like, and what functionality it is to include.

At this stage the prototype will typically not reflect all the validation and derivation rules (the invariants) to be specified in the information and function models. Many of these will emerge during the build stage. Also, because it is only worthwhile prototyping parts of the system which the user can see and which can be created automatically from the models by code generators, there will be parts of the functionality which will exist only as stub modules in the prototype.

Example:

Guest Registration

The Guest Administration System includes registering a guest, and the design prototype includes a facility to enter the guest's credit card number. However, the final system will integrate with a 'swipe' machine which will read the credit card details directly. This was not included in the prototype since it would not be cost effective and the requirement is clear and easily stated. What is included, however, is a call to a stub module that simply produces a documentary message. The stub will be replaced in the final system by the appropriate swipe machine interface module.

The section on "Stub Modules for Non-Prototyped Functionality" on page 70 discusses the use of stubs in prototypes more fully.

Figure 5-1 shows the use of a stub module in the design prototype for Guest Registration.

Figure 5-1

The Guest Registration Design Prototype

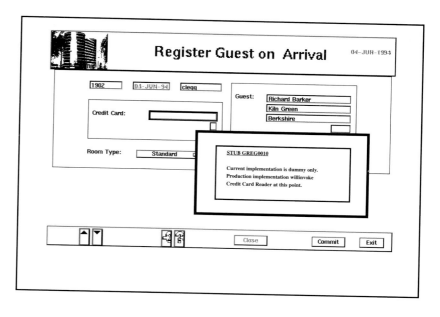

Critical Success Factors

As a result of the design prototype review there will be changes and additions to be made. These must be well documented and achievable in the time available. If insufficient detail of the requirements was defined in the workshops then there will be too much still to do. If the requirements were misunderstood in the workshops there will be too much rework to do. Even if the workshops were successful (sometimes because the workshops were so successful) the design prototype review is sometimes regarded as an opportunity to add further requirements. Ineffective workshops and unfocused design prototype reviews can leave the build stage with an impossible burden. Even if the build stage scope is correctly defined, it must still be distributed evenly amongst the resources available. If the partitions are unbalanced the whole project can be delayed unnecessarily.

The critical success factors can be summarized as:

- effective workshops
- successful design prototype
- balanced development partitions.

The Sub-stages and Tasks

The requirements stage consists of two major sub-stages – the completion of the definition of the requirements and the production and review of the design prototype. User interface design rules, usually known as the style guide or look and feel guidelines, may have been developed already for a previous project. Otherwise a style guide can be developed in parallel with defining the requirements.

Figure 5-2 below lists the tasks and sub-stages and Figure 5-3 opposite illustrates the dependencies between them. The tasks are defined in detail in the rest of this chapter.

Figure 5-2

List of Tasks

Sub-stage	Task
	Monitor and report progress, review and revise estimates and plans, quality check deliverables and control project
	Prototype look and feel requirements
Requirements Definition	Prepare for and conduct requirements workshops
	Consolidate and cross-consolidate requirements workshops
	Confirm project partitions
Design Prototype	Create default database design
	Create default application design
	Create default system architecture
	Generate design prototype
	Review design prototype
	Consolidate and document design prototype change requests
	Review, revise and sign off requirements

Figure 5-3

Sub-stages and Dependencies

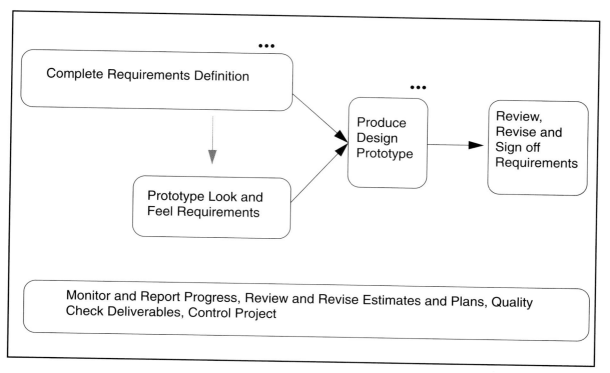

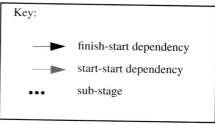

Tasks

TASK 1

Monitor and report progress, review and revise estimates and plans, quality check deliverables and control project

DESCRIPTION

All projects need to allow time and effort for administration. Fast-track projects are no different. This task ensures that the project runs smoothly and that progress is accurately and regularly reported to all interested parties.

Steps

1. Monitor and report progress regularly to team, users and sponsors.

2. Ensure project plan is maintained to reflect progress and expectations.

3. Ensure that deliverables are of acceptable quality.

4. Assign tasks and provide support and guidance to the team.

ESTIMATING: Expect less than two days a week. More indicates that the project is abnormally complex for a fast-track project, or the project administration is inefficient. Reassess the risk factors.

QUALITY: As a project gets more complex, the more difficult it becomes to evaluate the quality of the management, except with hindsight. Use simple indicators such as the timely arrival of the deliverables, changes to plan only as a result of external changes, and user and team satisfaction.

NOTES: Just as this task is a continuous one throughout the stage, so too, the steps are not sequential but represent ongoing responsibilities of the project manager and team.

In a fast-track project, day-to-day project management responsibilities are very likely to devolve to the team, of which one member will be the nominated project leader. The project leader should not be as heavily laden with development tasks as the rest of the team: for instance, he or she would probably have responsibility for development of the smallest partition. The project leader will not be a full-time administrator and the rest of the team should contribute to administration in such activities as progress reporting and peer-group quality checking without requiring management supervision. Even so, some time will be taken up with user meetings and 'number crunching'.

What might almost be classified as a deliverable of this task is the consistent high morale of the team – sometimes a time consuming deliverable to produce, and the techniques for doing so are beyond the scope of this book.

Since the requirements stage usually follows on directly from the planning stage, a separate briefing and kick-off task should not be necessary. See Task 5 in Chapter 4.

Deliverables

PREREQUISITES

– agreed project plan

- resource plan
- quality plan
- task schedule
- progress reporting standards

– deliverables from other tasks (for QA)

DELIVERABLES

– progress reports

– quality check results

– revised project plans

TECHNIQUES: Once the reporting mechanisms have been set in place measures of progress should be made regularly, probably weekly, and reported. If the progress is not as expected, action should be taken.

The objective in quality inspections is to quickly identify deliverables of dubious quality and concentrate time and effort on them, rather than expending the same level of effort across a much wider target area. Just as the good shepherd will *"...leave the ninety nine in the wilderness, and go after the one which is lost..."* (St. Luke 15:4), the good quality inspector will spend most time on exceptions!

As a result of progress monitoring it may be necessary to revise the project plan: see Chapter 2.

TOOLS: The critical success factor for time-efficient project progress monitoring and reporting is a good project control tool. Most of the effort in this task is in gathering actuals information, producing standard reports and disseminating these to a predetermined set of interested parties (team, users, sponsors etc.).

The critical success factor for time-efficient quality inspections is good CASE tool support. Use the Quality and Completeness Reports to highlight possible errors and omissions. Use the Matrix Diagrammer to display elementary functions against entities to check completeness (each entity should be used by at least one function for Create, Retrieve, Update and Delete) and to identify entities used by many functions, which are probably the most critical ones.

Tasks

TASK 2

Prototype look and feel requirements

DESCRIPTION

Before we can start to evolve solutions for users we need to develop standards for the appearance and behaviour of screens and reports, to improve usability and to diminish the need for rework during integration. This task delivers a definition of the standards for user interface design.

Steps

1. Evaluate any existing look and feel standards.

2. Create a partial/demonstration database.

3. Develop a set of suggested look and feel rules, based on existing standards or systems or based on experience.

4. Develop a number of prototype screens and reports to demonstrate suggested styles based on these rules.

5. Feed back prototypes to users and revise rules accordingly.

6. Redevelop prototypes and return to Step 4 if necessary.

7. Agree look and feel standards as a project style guide.

ESTIMATING: Time spent will be much less if we can agree to follow an existing standard rather than define one from scratch. Since the examples developed will be 'throw-aways', do not spend time developing the specifications.

QUALITY: The design rules should be acceptable to the users and easy to implement, preferably automatically in code generation. That is the goal.

NOTES: It is usually adequate to develop one data maintenance screen (preferably master/detail), one transaction screen (preferably multi-page and/or multi-window, which will demonstrate the different types of data that will be handled such as poplists, buttons, checkboxes etc.) and a two-level menu to demonstrate look and feel to users. If there are no existing style guides, try out different styles to see what is attractive to the users. Equivalently for reports, provide examples for summaries, details, reference data and transactional data.

When the Requirements Definition Sub-stage has been completed, you will have access to all the necessary function definitions to provide samples. However, by then this task will be on the critical path. It is better to take examples from the Requirements Definition Sub-stage as they emerge: it is not necessary that they are complete and reviewed, you only need examples. Similarly for the data definitions, a partial information model, which can be borrowed from the emerging requirements definitions, will be adequate.

If the database design that is used for the prototypes is to be discarded afterwards, there is no point adding the appearance and behaviour defaults to it, because these will be overwritten if we redefine the table definition as part of the requirements process (see pages 106 to 110).

Deliverables

PREREQUISITES

– example function definitions

– example information model

– existing style guides (if any)

DELIVERABLES

– project style guide
  - screens, menus, reports layout
  - list and validation processing
  - error handling
  - help delivery

– partial data appearance and behaviour defaults

– partial database design

– example implementations of the rules

TECHNIQUES: Whether or not we can implement the design rules automatically in code generation, it is still important to define the standards to which we are developing. Use prototypes or examples to ascertain user preferences and then formalize these as the style guide definition.

TOOLS: Use Oracle CASE Dictionary utilities to create a default database (probably a subset at this stage).

In the Oracle Generators, the design rules that make up the style guide are implemented as generator preferences in the Preferences Screen for the relevant generator and as defaults defined in Template Forms and Template Reports. Rules from both these sources are automatically applied by the generators. Data appearance and behaviour defaults are managed as part of Column Definitions in Oracle CASE Dictionary and then inherited by all generated modules that use the data. Data appearance and behaviour defaults include normal column sequence when a table is used, normal column display data type and size, and so on. However, see the notes opposite regarding the stability of such definitions, which may discarded if the database design proves to be unstable. For this reason it is best to delay fixing on the appearance and behaviour defaults at this time, where possible, because the partial database used for the prototype may well be discarded later. But users reviewing the prototypes will provide feedback, which should be documented as notes on the attribute from which the column is derived or as part of a specific document of database design notes. The Oracle CASE Dictionary provides a facility for users to define their own documents (which are maintained as text in the repository or as externally referenced files managed by some other text editor). These are very useful for checklist and 'to do' lists such as database design notes.

The Oracle Generators provide default facilities for list processing, error handling and help delivery. There are also facilities for developers to customize these if existing house standards demand. In the interests of efficiency it is better to accept the defaults wherever this is acceptable, but even if customization is needed, say a new help window, this is done only once and then reused many times.

Tasks

TASK 3
Prepare for and conduct requirements workshops

SUB-STAGE
Requirements Definition

DESCRIPTION

This task is the main source of detailed user input as to what the system is required to do.

Steps

1. Confirm partitions and priorities.
2. Arrange facilities.
3. Identify roles and brief participants.
4. Prepare material.
5. Conduct workshop.

ESTIMATING: Preparation time should not be more than a day, provided the team is familiar with the scope. Allow two days for the workshop with one facilitator and one scribe, and elapsed time beforehand to brief participants, arrange facilities and synchronize people's diaries.

QUALITY: The measures of quality will be successful completeness checks on the Oracle CASE Dictionary documentation, and the less tangible, but detectable, levels of user satisfaction and commitment.

NOTES: A requirements workshop should be timeboxed at two days. If this is not enough time, look for ways to repartition or to diminish the scope, using the priorities already agreed.

During the discussions you should encourage the use of real-world examples. You can ask users to bring examples to the workshops to discuss how they would be dealt with in the new system. These examples should be documented and references to them and other real-world examples kept as they will form the basis for realistic, but easily gathered, test data for use in the design prototype and beyond. Make sure they include some complex cases.

If the project was scoped by a workshop (see Task 2 of the Planning Stage on page 80) and has only one partition, a further requirements workshop may be unnecessary. There may already be sufficient detail in the requirements model to create a design prototype immediately.

Deliverables

PREREQUISITES

– requirements model

– partition definitions as subsets of the
requirements model

– partitions style definition (formal/iterative)

– user contacts for partitions

DELIVERABLES

– detailed requirements model
  • entity relationship model
  • function hierarchy (to elementary level)
  • entity to function cross-reference
  • list of business units involved
  • business unit to function cross-reference
  • event/function/key result cross-reference
    (optional)

– test data cases and test data references

TECHNIQUES: Workshops are a very demanding way of working at first, but they can be very productive when successful, and help build user and team commitment to a common goal.

The requirements workshops are seeking to deliver complete models to a level whereby a design prototype can be produced. This will involve all the major models (entity relationship diagrams, function hierarchy and/or dataflow diagrams).

See "Workshops for Requirements" on page 57, "Information Modelling" on page 38, "Function Modelling" on page 41 and "Systems Architecture Modelling" on page 44.

See also Techniques and Tools of Tasks 1 and 2 of the Planning Stage, pages 78 and 80.

TOOLS: The Oracle CASE tools provide facilities to create and revise the requirements model: the Function Hierarchy Diagrammer, Entity Relationship Diagrammer and Matrix Diagrammer. Matrices of event/function/key results can be constructed using user extensibility. Function definitions can be extended to include priority, and the Matrix Diagrammer used to display functions in order of priority.

Tasks

TASK 4

Consolidate and cross-consolidate requirements workshops

DESCRIPTION

A project may include one or more requirements workshops. Each one has the same format. If there is more than one, this task consolidates any changes that have impact across the boundaries.

Steps

1. Identify changes that affect more than one partition.

SUB-STAGE

Requirements Definition

2. Resolve cross-partition impact.

3. Complete documentation.

ESTIMATING: Allow a day for consolidation after the workshop. Less time, but not none, will be needed if the CASE tools have been used 'live'. If there is more than one workshop, resolving cross-partition impacts may take up to another day, assuming that all the models are in a single CASE repository and that the scribes of all the partitions can spend the time together. If there have been multiple workshops, it is wise to allow some time to consult with users again (informally) to resolve any clashes, probably only a half day, but take into account user availability, which may affect elapsed time more dramatically than effort.

QUALITY: Use Completeness Reports and Consistency Reports, in Oracle CASE Dictionary and Matrix Diagrams.

NOTES: After a requirements workshop, even one in which the CASE tools were used actively, there will be consolidation and consistency and completeness checking to be done. In the course of this work, impact analysis may indicate that function definitions and/or information definitions used in other partitions (which had been the subject of other workshops) require changes. Both these classes of changes need to be tracked, resolved and documented. In a single-partition project this task only involves writing up the notes from the workshop, if any are still outstanding.

Deliverables

PREREQUISITES

– requirements model
  (from all the requirements workshops)

DELIVERABLES

– requirements model
  (consolidated, from all the requirements workshops)

TECHNIQUES: The techniques in use here are a combination of quality checking and completeness checking, which to a large extent can be automated by standard repository reports and the resolution of inconsistencies and gaps. Inconsistencies can be caused by simple documentary slips or could be more fundamental.

An example of a simple slip is where conflicts in domain definitions may be caused by one set of users providing a slightly different set of valid values. This is easily resolved. An example of a more fundamental error is where one set of users requires a piece of information and the users responsible for the function that produces that information do not specify it as a deliverable from their activities. This kind of impasse may require further consultation with users.

See also "Workshops for Requirements" on page 57.

TOOLS: Oracle CASE Dictionary Quality and Completeness Reports provide an indicator of inconsistencies and gaps.

The Matrix Diagrammer is particularly useful to identify missing usages (information and business unit). Every elementary business function should be performed by at least one business unit and should use at least one entity. Every business unit should perform at least one function. Every entity should be created, retrieved, updated (possibly) and deleted by at least one elementary function.

Tasks

TASK 5

Confirm project partitions

DESCRIPTION

After the workshops and consolidation, the basis for the decisions made during the planning stage about the scope of the different partitions may have changed. This task reassesses the partition boundaries and contents.

Steps

1. Assess need to reconsider partitioning; if no significant corrections were made in Task 4, this task is not necessary.

SUB-STAGE

Requirements Definition

2. Reapply partitioning rules.

3. Review and agree revisions to partition definitions.

ESTIMATING: Usually nothing! If the task needs doing it will correspond to Task 4 of the Planning Stage.

QUALITY: See Task 4 of the Planning Stage on page 84.

NOTES: This task is here to remind the project manager that the partitions can change. This may have occurred as a result of revisions to the dependencies between functions identified and corrected in Task 4. If the partitions are not redefined then they may no longer be optimally bounded in terms of their cohesion and coupling, and they may not represent balanced work packages for the team.

If partitioning has to be redone, it does not need to delay design prototyping. However, the team members will probably prefer to be responsible for producing the design prototypes of the facilities that they will eventually be responsible for developing in full, so it is best done at this point if possible.

Deliverables

PREREQUISITES

- partition definitions as subsets of the requirements model
- partitions style definition (formal/iterative)
- user contacts for partitions
- cost estimates
- project risk assessment

DELIVERABLES

- revised partition definitions as subsets of the requirements model
- revised partitions style definition
- revised user contacts for partitions
- revised cost estimates
- revised project risk assessment

TECHNIQUES:

TOOLS: See Task 4 of the Planning Stage on page 84.

Tasks

TASK 6
*Create default
database design*

DESCRIPTION

This task creates a database definition on which the design prototype will be built.

Steps

1. Review the database definitions created for the look and feel prototype; delete if unwanted.

SUB-STAGE
Design Prototype

2. Map all remaining entities in the scope of the implementation onto tables as required.

3. Produce a default database design of tables, columns and keys.

4. Review and revise physical database default.

5. Define additional invariant data rules based on informal specifications at entity and attribute level.

6. Specify column appearance and behaviour defaults.

ESTIMATING: This task is mostly automated; it should take little time to run the default database design. If additional data invariant rules have been captured at requirements time, they should be formalized here if possible. Allow a little time for reviewing the column behaviour defaults, although these will be subject to user review later. See estimation under Task 8 on page 116.

QUALITY: The effort should be concentrated on the formalization of invariant definitions. Much of the remainder only represents a transformation of information gathered in the requirements definition sub-stage, which should have been quality checked then.

NOTES: In Task 2 you may have created some database definitions. The subsequent requirements workshops may well have added to, or modified, the entities and attributes on which they are based, in which case it is easier to delete these tables and let the CASE tools redesign the database.

It is probably better not to produce the index design at this point. The volumes of data being used in design prototyping are unlikely to benefit from indexes and maintaining the design will occupy resources. Index design is better delayed until integration (see Task 15 of the Build Stage on page 160 and "Performance Trials" on page 167).

For a design prototype, it is not necessary to concern yourself with decisions about where validation is performed and constraints are checked (client side or server side). Tuning can wait until later.

Deliverables

PREREQUISITES

– information model
  • entity relationship model

DELIVERABLES

– information model
  • schema definition
        tables
        columns
        invariants (partial)
        default appearance & behaviour
        (unreviewed)
– default physical database design
  (from default schema with defaulted physical
  implementation details)

TECHNIQUES: The derivation of a normalized database design from an accurate entity relationship model is a well-understood process (see Appendix F of Barker, 1990). For the purposes of a design prototype, it is not necessary to refine the database design for performance optimization or data distribution. In a fast-track project performance tuning should be left until and unless testing indicates that it is necessary.

See also "Information Modelling" on page 38.

TOOLS: The Oracle CASE Dictionary Default Database Design Utility will perform the bulk of this task automatically.

Column constraints and validation are defined in Oracle CASE Dictionary as structured text items associated with a column definition, and default appearance and behaviour are defined as column properties, both via the Column Definition Screen. Table constraints are defined as text items via the Keys and Constraints Screen of Oracle CASE Dictionary. All these definitions are inherited by modules subsequently defined to use the relevant columns and tables, and the Oracle Generator for Forms implements them in the generated code. The Oracle CASE Dictionary Data Definition Language (DDL) Generator also (or alternatively) generates constraints as server-side declaratives or as client-side triggers, hence enforcing data integrity in the database.

Tasks

TASK 7 *Create default* *application design*	**DESCRIPTION** This task defines the processing modules that will be implemented in the design prototype.

TASK 7

Create default
application design

DESCRIPTION

This task defines the processing modules that will be implemented in the design prototype.

Steps

1. Create default module definitions for facilities to support all elementary functions within the scope of the project.

2. Check that all expected data usages have been implemented.

SUB-STAGE

Design Prototype

3. Specify the data navigation for each module.

ESTIMATING: If this task is supported by CASE tools, it can be mostly automated and should not take long to complete. See estimation under Task 8 on page 116.

QUALITY: You could take the time to check the design documentation of each module by hand. However, just as for the database design, since these have been produced automatically from the requirements definitions, the quality assurance should have been part of the requirements definition process.

NOTES: Step 2 of this task is really part of the quality assurance for the design; however, since it can have considerable impact on the project, it is treated as a separate step. Where a function uses certain attributes of an entity, the facility that supports that function can be expected to use the corresponding columns of the table that implements that entity. If the table has been excluded from the database design (step 2 of Task 6), this may be a simple error, in which case it is easily corrected. If it represents a genuine confusion about the scope of the project, it may not be so easily resolved. For example, the entity may be implemented in an existing system. If the data is in a different database from the one on which the current project is to be implemented, we will need to specify another facility. This facility will either access the data directly in the foreign data source, or copy it across into a mirror table in the current system. Either way, the development has become more complex and has acquired an external dependency. If the table is implemented in the current database, as part of a previous project, then its definition should be made available to this project for reuse.

Requirements models define what data is to be used; they do not specify how. For example, a module that examines the history of a frequent guest, enquiring on Guest records and Visit records, might first find the Guest record and then show the dates and location (which hotel) for each visit. Alternatively, it might identify the hotel and then the dates, finally displaying guest details. Which is the correct data navigation route for a module is not obvious from the data usages, but it must be specified as part of the module definition.

Deliverables

PREREQUISITES

– function model

 • function hierarchy (to elementary level)
 • entity to function cross-reference

DELIVERABLES

– revised function model

 • systems facilities model
 • module definition
 • table usages
 • column usages
 • facility-specific processing
   (initial specification)

TECHNIQUES: Having prototyped the look and feel requirements to create a style guide for the user interface, and defaulted the appearance and behaviour of the data in creating the default database design (Task 6), default application design need not concern itself with user interface design for the modules. The task is to identify suitable modules to support the business functions. This should concentrate on identifying the appropriate type of support (screen, report, background utility) and specifying any additional facility-specific processing that was identified in requirements analysis.

See also "Function Modelling" on page 41.

TOOLS: The Oracle CASE Dictionary Default Application Design Utility will perform the bulk of this task. It will identify candidate modules and document data usages of tables and columns to correspond to the usages of entities, attributes and relationships specified for the function or functions from which each module is derived.

Additional facility-specific validation can be entered as text items associated with column usages: data derivations can be specified as additional column usages; access restrictions can be specified as text items associated with table usages; all of these are entered as Detailed Data Usages in Oracle CASE Dictionary.

Overrides to the appearance and behaviour defaults can also be recorded in the Detailed Data Usages Screen, but it is usually unnecessary and unproductive to do this before user review of the design prototype.

The data navigation can be specified via the Data Usages Linking facility in the Oracle Generators.

Tasks

TASK 8
*Create default
system architecture*

SUB-STAGE
Design Prototype

DESCRIPTION

This task defines the menu modules and other structural links that will be implemented in the design prototype.

Steps

1. For each group of users involved (business units), create a menu and an overall system menu to invoke the user menus.

2. For each module identified, attach it to the menu belonging to any business unit that performs the function that the module supports.

3. Split menus that are regarded as too full and/or split modules by type.

4. Order modules according to data dependencies and likely usage patterns.

5. Link modules together to represent policy (function dependencies).

ESTIMATING: The system architecture may well change substantially at review and so preparation of the default design should not be allowed to take a great deal of effort. Try to complete the default design of database, application and architecture in two days or less using the whole team. If it takes more, perhaps the scope is too large or you are spending too much time on unnecessary detail.

QUALITY: The quality will tell only when the prototype is reviewed. This is true for all aspects of the design prototype, but particularly for the architecture, which is driven almost entirely by the user interface and hence is subject to the users' preferences.

NOTES: The design approach suggested here is very simplistic. However, it has the advantage that it is easy to achieve quickly and is easy to implement. Reviewing the design prototype (see Task 10) will provide input directly from the users about how they want it improved. To keep up the fast-track pace, it is probably better to stick to a simpler interface design, which is easy to implement, than to spend user and designer time in creating the optimal design, which is then much more difficult to implement. If there is time left later to tweak the design, well and good.

What is regarded as the best arrangement of menus and modules is fairly arbitrary. The look and feel prototype should provide guidelines, but the users may change their minds when they see the whole system assembled (in skeletal form) in the design prototype.

If there are modules that will not be generated for the design prototype, for example background utilities, but which are significant to the overall structure and operation of the system, they may be represented at this stage by a 'stub' module to indicate the point at which the utility would be invoked. The use of stub modules is discussed in "Stub Modules for Non-Prototyped Functionality" on page 70.

Deliverables

PREREQUISITES

– architecture model

- function hierarchy (to elementary level)
- entity to function cross-reference
- list of business units involved
- business unit to function cross-reference
- event/function/key result cross-reference (if available)

DELIVERABLES

– architecture model

- menu definitions
- invocations of facilities from other facilities (menu to menu, menu to screen, report, etc.)

TECHNIQUES: From the default application design (Task 7) you will have a collection of modules (screens, reports, etc.). The system architecture will define how these are to fit together, and define the menus needed to provide default access to them. The architecture will also define who the users are and what access rights they are to have to the facilities. For the purposes of the design prototype it is not necessary to specify roles and users. In a fast-track project these are often not necessary at all. Since it is likely that the project is for a relatively homogeneous user population, in all probability they will all have the same access. Default architecture creation should aim to deliver a simple structure that users can quickly grasp and navigate. A simple menu hierarchy is usually the best starting place. If other navigational requirements are known (from function dependencies) these can be defined as module to module calls. More requirements of this nature will emerge in the design prototype review and beyond, which will necessitate changes.

See also "Systems Architecture Modelling" on page 44.

TOOLS: The Oracle CASE Dictionary Default Menu Design Utility will perform the bulk of this task. It will identify and define menus for each of the business units that perform at least one of the functions that are to be supported by the facilities of the system, and will associate the appropriate modules (screens etc.) with each business unit's menu. The utility uses rules (which may have been modified by the look and feel prototype) to make decisions about whether to split menus that get too large.

Modifications to the architecture can be made via Oracle CASE Dictionary's Module Network Screen.

TASK 9
Generate design prototype

DESCRIPTION
This task transforms the design specified in Tasks 6, 7 and 8 above.

Steps

1. Generate database definition.

2. Generate menu system.

3. Generate database maintenance modules.

SUB-STAGE
Design Prototype

4. Test the data maintenance modules and create test data.

5. Generate and test the data detail reports.

6. Generate and test transactional screen modules.

7. Generate and test remaining reports.

8. Implement test harness for background-invoked modules as required.

9. Implement stub modules for background processing modules.

ESTIMATING: If it took two days to default the design, then it will probably take three to five days to generate it, create a small set of test data and test the prototype.

QUALITY: The most common error in generating the design prototype is to forget to create part of the prototype or to ignore data dependencies, so the team is constantly having to go back to fix problems which should not have existed. Generating the design prototype is almost like running an entire development in three days. If the process is sound, the results will be sound.

NOTES: Without CASE tool support it becomes difficult to justify the design prototype in a fast-track project. The traditional approach would be to have the users review the outline designs, on the basis of written definitions, diagrams, and screen and report layouts. The design prototype provides a much more effective medium for user review, but only if it can be created swiftly, directly from the design specifications. It will change quite considerably in the review, and the code created will be thrown away in most cases. Since new code can be easily generated for the revised designs, the effort is not wasted because the designs themselves are reusable and evolvable even though the generated code is thrown away.

It is impossible to test a transaction or a report without any data. The easiest way to ensure that there is valid test data is when it has been entered by the maintenance screens for the system. The maintenance screens should be generated first. That is the reason that the steps are defined and ordered as they are. There may be occasions when you will need to build extra reports and/or screens to enter test data or to review it. This will occur when the system gets its data by batch load from another system or when the system does not include reports of all the data it contains.

Deliverables

PREREQUISITES	DELIVERABLES

PREREQUISITES

– design specification
  • schema definition
  • systems facilities model
  • menu definitions
  • invocations of facilities from other facilities
– test data cases and test data references

DELIVERABLES

– design prototype
  • physical database
  • menus
  • screens
  • reports
  • stub modules
– extended test data

TECHNIQUES: A design prototype is highly unlikely to be created in full without CASE tools and generator technology.

See "Prototyping" on page 61.

Although it is not the primary objective of this task to produce test data, some test data is necessary; it should be produced in a format that can be reused in reviewing the prototype with users (Task 10) and in integration testing later. Build on the test cases from Task 3; this saves time and produces realistic test data.

See "Test Planning and Testing" on page 33.

TOOLS: The Oracle Generator for Forms and the Oracle Generator for Reports provide the capabilities you need to create a design prototype. You should resist the temptation to customize the generated modules before user review unless it is necessary to illustrate a critical aspect of the whole system. If the look and feel generally seems unlikely to be acceptable there may be a case for revising the style guide, and re-examining the QA process on Task 2. If there are one or two modules with complex layouts for which the style guide does not provide usable designs, it is probably better to leave them anyway until later. Layout may be altered by subsequent design changes (for example, inclusion of additional data, exclusion of existing data, changes to appearance and behaviour, changes to structure). The Oracle Generator for Forms can re-generate a module to modify most aspects of its operation and will not affect the layout (including any customization), but all the types of changes listed above may imply layout changes. If this has already been customized by hand the generator cannot modify it; it can only replace it, which will mean either repeating the customization on a new version or implementing by hand the changes that the generator could have implemented automatically.

Tasks

TASK 10 *Review design prototype*	**DESCRIPTION** The design prototype is the first substantial deliverable from the project. This task provides the users (sponsor and stakeholders) with the opportunity to examine and critique it.

TASK 10

Review design prototype

DESCRIPTION

The design prototype is the first substantial deliverable from the project. This task provides the users (sponsor and stakeholders) with the opportunity to examine and critique it.

Steps

1. Arrange review and brief participants.

2. Prepare test cases.

SUB-STAGE

Design Prototype

3. Conduct design prototype walkthrough.

4. Document and confirm requested changes.

5. Identify sources of further valid test data.

6. Agree status of design.

ESTIMATING: This may well be the first opportunity the users have had to 'get their hands on' the system, which means that productivity will be lower, especially to start with, whilst users become familiar with it. Allow one day learning time plus one day per partition (that is at least two days).

QUALITY: If the review fails to reach a conclusion in the desired time one or more of the following three things has happened: the team has not used the review techniques properly, the team has not produced an accurate requirements specification or the users have changed their minds. Probably a bit of all of them. Only the first cause arises within this task. The key to a successful review is not only quality prerequisites but good use of the techniques. Try to ensure that the team has adequate preparation and confidence.

NOTES: If the project has more than one partition, the design can be reviewed by partition. The advantage is that users only need to be present for the feedback sessions that concern them. The disadvantage is that some controversial issues may arise that cannot be resolved in the session, which will increase the load in consolidation and the probability that a re-review of at least part of the design will be necessary. Where possible, the best solution is to stage one review, divide it into sessions, invite the appropriate users to each session and invite all users to the final session where any outstanding issues can be aired and resolved. This is the most difficult way and the most draining for the team, but all the issues are raised and dealt with whilst they are fresh in people's minds, giving this approach the best chance of success in the minimum timescale.

As part of the final session, the consolidation, be sure to identify all the work to be done. If CASE tools were available in the review, it may have been possible to revise designs and generate a new prototype for some of the necessary changes. Where this has not been done, summarize the changes requested and whether or not they will need to be re-reviewed. If they need reviewing, identify who will review them, and when.

There is an opportunity to really get user buy-in to the process during the review. Use it. There is also the risk of alienating the users, by not reflecting their needs in the prototype or by appearing to be unwilling to do so.

Deliverables

PREREQUISITES

– design prototype

- menus
- screens
- reports
- stub modules

– test data

DELIVERABLES

– revised design prototype

– revised design specification

- schema definition
- systems facilities model
- menu definitions
- invocations of facilities from other facilities

– change requests to design specification

– expanded test data

TECHNIQUES: One of the most successful prototype review styles is where the developer has the CASE workbench and the stakeholder has a terminal or workstation of the type that will be used for the implemented system attached. This may be the same as the developer's workstation. With this configuration the stakeholder can actually operate the prototype and the developer can note the changes directly in the CASE tools. Some changes can be implemented 'live' and retested in the same session. This is very effective for building the stakeholder's confidence in, and ownership of, the system, but it requires a high level of skills in the developer, who may need to be generating one part of the prototype in response to a requested change, whilst at the same time taking notes on the changes required to the next part of the prototype.

The review of the design prototype should pay particular attention to the definition of the data and its rules. During build, changes to shared data definitions will have cross-partition effects, and will hence be more expensive to fix. Try, as far as is possible, to stabilize the database design at this stage.

See also "Prototype and Build Iteration Reviews" on page 66.

TOOLS: Even if the developer is not using the CASE tools to implement changes 'live', the CASE tools should be used during the review to document the changes. Directly entering the changes provides a reminder of all the information required. For example, if we need to define a new validation constraint, then entering this directly as a table constraint will remind the developer to ask what the error message should be and whether the constraint should be enforced at the server or client or both.

Any and all of the Oracle CASE tools may be needed.

Tasks

TASK 11

Consolidate and document design prototype change requests

DESCRIPTION

This task ensures that all user change requests from the prototype review are either implemented or documented as outstanding.

Steps

1. Identify changes to look and feel guidelines, resolve clashes and document.

2. Identify changes to data definitions, appearance and behaviour, resolve clashes and document.

3. Identify additions and changes to system architecture structure, document and generate new prototypes.

4. Identify changes and additions to each module's appearance and processing, document and generate new prototypes.

5. Re-review if necessary.

SUB-STAGE

Design Prototype

ESTIMATING: It is not necessarily a bad thing if there are many changes at this stage. Changes at this stage take minutes or hours: later they may take hours and days. Allow the team two full days each, and hope you will not need them. If you do need them, a re-review is probably necessary, but there will be less need for familiarization this time and less ground to cover than in the original review. Allow half a day per partition for re-review.

QUALITY: The consolidation session of the design prototype review should have produced a list of outstanding changes. Check it against the memory of the participants and against the revised prototype.

NOTES: Make the changes to the elements that will be reused first – Steps 1 and 2. The diagram below shows the dependencies between the steps:

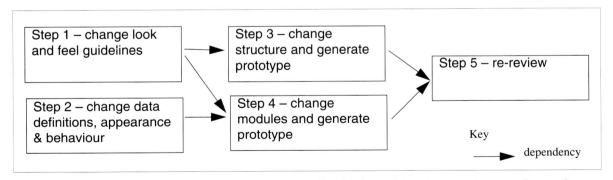

Many of the changes will be filling in details of rules and invariants, stating a preference for user interface, or correcting misapprehensions, but some will be 'scope creep'. These should be identified and their impact understood. They should probably be assigned a lower priority in the project plan.

Deliverables

PREREQUISITES

(for each partition)

– design specification

– design prototype

– change requests to design specification

DELIVERABLES

– revised design prototype

– revised design specifications

– revised project priorities

TECHNIQUES: With a design prototype we should aim for one review only. The objective is not to produce the final system at this stage, but to identify broadly the characteristics that it will have when it is built. So it should not be necessary to go back and re-review changes.

This rule may be broken, either because the sheer volume of changes requested is so high that the prototype cannot be said to have captured the characteristics of the system, or because the consolidation session identifies some far-reaching implications of a change which will need to be approved by the sponsor and stakeholders.

See also "Prototype and Build Iteration Reviews" on page 66.

TOOLS: The Matrix Diagrammer can be used for impact analysis to identify which changes affect other partitions, and how.

Where changes affect existing prototypes these should be re-created with the generators to establish that the changes are as intended.

TASK 12

Review, revise and sign off requirements

DESCRIPTION

This task ensures that users, management and team all agree what the system will deliver and that the requirements definition and project plan reflect this clearly and accurately.

Steps

1. Arrange sign-off meeting and brief sponsor.

2. Review project scope and priorities.

3. Review project plan, timescales, resources and costs.

4. Revise plans and priorities as required to get agreement.

ESTIMATING: One short meeting with the sponsor or sponsors should be adequate. A fast-track project is founded on the assumption that we have the right people for the job, the right users with authority to specify needs, the right team to capture those needs accurately. Hence this sign-off procedure should be a formality. If it is not, then the project is at risk and should be reviewed as a whole.

QUALITY: See above: either the user sponsor will be satisfied or the project is in trouble.

NOTES: The requirements sign-off is the single most significant project milestone. After this the main effort of development will be in the build stage. There should be no doubt as to the goals, objectives and priorities of the project after this meeting.

As part of the review process you may want to demonstrate the design prototype more widely. Now is a good time to get the buy-in of other influencers in the user community but be sure that they understand that what is demonstrated is only a prototype.

Deliverables

PREREQUISITES

(consolidated for all partitions)

– design specification

– design prototype

– change requests to design specification

– prioritization of function requirements

– agreed project plan
  • resource plan
  • quality plan
  • task schedule
  • progress reporting standards

DELIVERABLES

– revised design prototype

– revised design specifications

– revised prioritization of function requirements

– revised project plan

TECHNIQUES: Having project management tools with what-if analysis capability available can reduce the need for further meetings if revisions are needed, because the project manager can make the changes during the meeting and try out alternative plans.

Use the design prototype in the review to remind the sponsor what is being discussed and particularly to resolve any confusion about relative priorities *"Is it more important to include this... or this..?"*

See also Task 8 of the Planning Stage on page 92.

TOOLS: The use of CASE tools in the meeting itself may help because comments can be captured directly, for example, changes to priority.

The Matrix Diagrammer provides a good interface for reviewing and revising project priorities. The module specifications (Module Definition, Module Network and Module Detailed Data Usage Screens) and even the prototypes can be useful for confirming that particular points are represented in the system definition.

Summary

In the requirements stage the scope that was agreed during planning is fleshed out and defined more precisely. The sponsor, stakeholders and developers will have agreed what the system is going to look like from the design prototype and who is responsible for which parts of it from the partition definitions, and they will have a fairly firm idea of how long it is going to take. These are the tangibles. Less tangible, but just as important, will be the vision this extended team of users and systems people will share of what they want, and how they will achieve it. Success depends on a strong team spirit, and the requirements stage, where sponsor, stakeholders and developers work together in workshops and reviews, is the opportunity to forge unity of purpose and high motivation.

6

BUILD STAGE

Overview

Traditionally, the build stage is one where not only the users but also the business analysts become detached from the process, which now plunges into technology, hopefully to emerge at the end as the system that was required. In fast-track the process is very different: business analysts, armed with CASE tools and generator technology, side by side with the users, continue to drive the technology, not the other way round. However, because there will be areas that require in-depth knowledge of specialized technology, such as our earlier example of the credit card swipe, the build stage will introduce a new role – the implementation specialist – who will usually work on a particular project partition to develop or customize complex processing. Occasionally, as with the swipe, a whole partition may be run as a non-user-driven build sub-project, and the leader would then be an implementation specialist, with the business analyst in a consultative role and the user involved at integration testing.

Objectives

In the build stage our objectives are:

- to maximize productivity
- to ensure that the developed system matches the original requirement.

The requirement is expressed by the user reviewers for each partition and by the overall requirements model and design prototype. The best way to combine these is to use CASE tools and code generators as much as possible to produce the system.

Major Deliverables

During the build stage there will be amendments and additions to the models produced in the requirements stage to reflect changes required by the users and the addition of detail to specify the system precisely. The build stage also produces most of the components of the final system:

- code and implemented database
- user documentation

and other deliverables that are used in later stages:

- test plans, test data and test results for acceptance testing
- system development documentation for maintenance

and most importantly, though intangible:

- user acceptance of the developed system.

Code and Implemented Database

These represent the primary objectives of the project. Where the implementation is not totally re-creatable from the CASE environment, that is, where it is not totally generated,. additional documentation may be required. No additional implementation documentation of generated code is necessary.

End-user Documentation

This normally takes the form of online help, which is a less exacting requirement than some projects deliver. However, it is a reasonable goal for a fast-track project, where the level of knowledge of the working system will be much higher among the end-user population at system installation than would be the case with a more traditional approach.

Test Plans, Test Data and Test Results

If there is to be additional user acceptance testing during the transition to the use of the new system, the test scenarios and data developed in the build stage for module and for integration testing will be reused as the basis of the acceptance test. They may also form the basis of regression tests during maintenance and be used in developing user training.

System Development Documentation

Normally this will be the contents of the CASE repository at the conclusion of the development. The design-level models that directly drive the code generators will need to be kept up to date. Documentation of any code developed outside the CASE environment may be needed for maintenance later. Usually the only system development documentation that is necessary in a fast-track project is the design specification and the original requirements workshops results, prior to the development of the design prototype. The original business-level specifications need only be maintained during the build stage if there is a major change, for example, in scope.

User Acceptance

Whilst there may be further testing before final implementation of the system (see "User Training and Acceptance Testing" on page 165), by the end of the build stage all the components of the system and the overall integration and behaviour should have been seen and approved by stakeholders.

Critical Success Factors

Once a build stage is in progress the biggest threat to success is change. But change is inevitable, so the critical success factors of the build stage are concerned with either resisting change or, more usually, controlling it. One source of change is the user review. Stakeholders will identify new requirements (scope creep) and they will change their minds about how a particular requirement should best be implemented (flip-flop). Such changes are inevitable, but each one should be challenged (*"If we don't include this will the system fail?"*) and if it is genuinely necessary, then its priority should be carefully assessed (*"If we include X then Y will have to be moved off the 'should have' list onto the 'could have' list. Is X really more important than Y?"*).

When changes are accepted they may well impact other partitions and the build iterations have a task built into them to consolidate these changes. However, the sooner developers know about changes that affect them, the less work they have to do to accommodate the changes. Good team working and communication are essential. As a developer, whenever you need to make a change that will affect someone else, ask yourself, *"Can I make this change in a way that will minimize or eliminate the impact on others?"* and *"Can I delay making the change until a time that's convenient for everyone concerned?"*, and keep the team informed.

The critical success factors can be summarized as:

- little or no scope creep and requirements flip-flop
- ruthless management of project priorities
- well-documented and well-communicated cross-partition change requests.

The Sub-stages and Tasks

The major deliverables of the build stage will be the software itself and whatever documentation was agreed as part of the project plan; for example, user help, test plans and CASE repository definitions. Not all of these will be required for all projects so the task plan will be amended accordingly. As with the other stages, the task definitions in the remainder of the chapter provide a template from which an individual project plan can be constructed.

Figure 6-1 below lists the tasks and sub–stages and Figure 6-2 illustrates the dependencies between them. The tasks are defined in detail in the rest of this chapter.

Figure 6-1
List of Tasks

Sub-stage	Task
	Monitor and report progress, review and revise estimates and plans, quality check deliverables and control project
	Confirm partitions and initiate the build stage
Iterate Build and User Review	Build and revise system components
	Review system components with users
	Collate external changes
	Implement external changes
Conduct Formal Build	Prepare test plans and data
	Develop and test a code milestone
	Collate external changes
	Implement external changes
	Produce online help etc.
	Quality check code and testing process
	Prepare for integration test
Integrate Components	Conduct integration test
	Review test results and rework
	Conduct integration retest

Figure 6-2

Sub-stages and dependencies

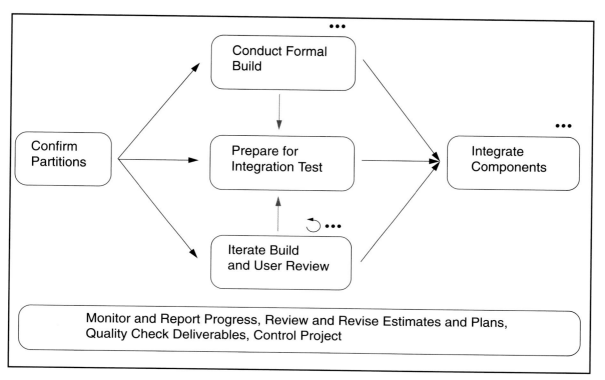

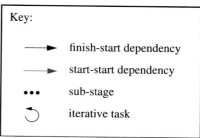

Key:

→	finish-start dependency
→	start-start dependency
•••	sub-stage
↺	iterative task

Tasks

TASK 1

Monitor and report progress, review and revise estimates and plans, quality check deliverables and control project

DESCRIPTION

This task ensures that the project runs smoothly and that progress is accurately and regularly reported to all interested parties.

Steps

1. Monitor and report progress regularly to team, users and sponsors.

2. Ensure project plan is maintained to reflect progress and expectations.

3. Ensure that deliverables are of acceptable quality.

4. Assign tasks and provide support and guidance to the team.

ESTIMATING: Progress reporting should be routine by this stage of the project; however, QA activities may well increase, as will support and guidance to the team, especially if new implementation specialists have joined. As a general rule, a six-person team means that the team leader is occupied full time by project administration. Fast-track build stages do better than this because the team members are experienced enough to work unaided. Senior developers should share quality check duties. A target of half time on project control and half on build activities is reasonable, with quality checking shared between the developers, taking no more than five percent of their time.

QUALITY: As project leader you will need to keep a close watch on your own time management and productivity. Adjust the load sooner rather than allowing the project to become unsynchronized and delayed.

NOTES: Quality checking of the user interface is being done by the users. Generated code should not need testing, only the rules it implements. Documentation standards in code should be enforced automatically by the generators. Design documentation is usually only what is necessarily produced for the generators to run from. The major QA requirement is to ensure that change requests are managed and documented properly.

Deliverables

PREREQUISITES

– project plan

- resource plan

- quality plan

- task schedule

- progress reporting standards

– deliverables from other tasks (for QA)

DELIVERABLES

– results of quality checks

– progress reports

– revised project plan

TECHNIQUES: Quality checks for non-generated code are different from the checks we do on automatically generated code that has been user tested and approved. Task 12 on page 154 has been introduced to reflect this special requirement and is in addition to other QA activity, not a replacement for it.

Even in fast-track projects, maybe especially in fast-track projects, attention to quality issues in planning and conduct of the project will save excessive fix time later. Provided we check the things that are likely to go wrong, rather than blanket double-checking of everything we do, we can raise quality assurance without lowering productivity at build time, and in the maintenance cycle the effort will be more than repaid.

See "Prototype and Build Iteration Reviews" on page 66.

TOOLS: Use the Module History Screen or create Documents associated with modules, tables and the application in Oracle CASE Dictionary for change tracking if required. Using Documents imposes no structure; they are just free text associated with an element in the Dictionary. Using Module History allows better control and tracking although this latter approach is probably unnecessarily bureaucratic for a fast-track project.

Use the reports from Oracle CASE Dictionary to check quality and completeness of database and module designs.

Tasks

TASK 2

Confirm partitions and initiate the build stage

DESCRIPTION

The build stage may well introduce new members of the team, specifically implementation specialists and a wider group of user stakeholders, so it is worthwhile briefly reviewing the plans and briefing the team. That is the purpose of this task.

Steps

1. Review project plan and confirm milestones.

2. Identify suitable resources for each partition, revise the scope of partitions as necessary.

3. Identify user representatives with review authority for each partition.

4. Identify user representative with project coordination responsibility.

5. Brief participants.

ESTIMATING: If the original team of developers and users is unchanged at this stage, there is no need for a briefing as the roles will already be known. If the requirements stage has gone to plan, this task is little more than a formality which should not occupy much time. However, if there are changes in scope, priorities and personnel, then the time taken here, up to two days effort with perhaps a week elapsed by the time briefings have been arranged and conducted, will be repaid in the smoother running of the build stage.

QUALITY: The objective is to ensure that everyone involved knows how the build stage will proceed and what is expected of them. And also what is **not** expected of them – those really neat 'bells and whistles' that do not help the business and the user has not asked for may take a significant amount of time to implement. If all the guidelines are followed then the only measure is, unfortunately, hindsight.

NOTES: When assigning partitions and reviewing partition scope, bear in mind the need to synchronize reviews in order to manage external changes more easily. There may be a need to balance cohesion and coupling against development time.

As well as users with the knowledge and authority to review build iterations and accept them when complete, we will need to identify one user representative as project coordinator. She or he will be authorized to resolve any conflict that may arise from a change in one partition affecting another. This may be the project sponsor, but he or she may not have sufficient in-depth knowledge of the operations to perform this task unaided.

Deliverables

PREREQUISITES

– project plan
– partition definitions
– user contacts for partitions

DELIVERABLES

– reviewed project plan
  • reviewed resource plan
  • reviewed task schedule
– revised partition definitions
– revised user contacts for partitions

TECHNIQUES: This task has two elements. One is reviewing and revising plans and schedules. The second, and more important for the project manager, is communicating the plans and tasks. Although tools can be used, for example, distributing project plans by electronic mail, the challenge is to ensure that all participants genuinely understand the importance of their part in making the whole project work. In a tight schedule, typical of fast-track projects, a single person missing one user review or other project meeting can easily delay the whole project.

See "Partitioning the Project" on page 21 and Task 2 in the Requirements Stage.

TOOLS: Oracle CASE tools manage the information concerning the project content (module definitions, partitions, etc.).

Tasks

TASK 3
Build and revise system components

DESCRIPTION

In this task a developer takes a group of modules, representing a partition of the system, and based on the design prototype and the outstanding changes from that, evolves the implementation to a state where it can be reviewed by the stakeholders. The final objective is to arrive at a coherent and complete set of modules accepted by the stakeholders, such that any outstanding changes are not regarded as necessary or worth the effort of implementing them.

SUB-STAGE
Iterate Build and User Review

Steps

1. Classify outstanding changes as module specific or database.

2. Investigate possible external implications of database changes.

3. Group changes by subject (database table, module, etc.).

4. Order changes by dependencies (internal and external).

5. Implement and test changes unit by unit.

6. Document user help and error-handling text.

ESTIMATING: Allow four weeks maximum for the first iteration, although three weeks will probably be sufficient; second and subsequent iterations (if needed) should take progressively less time (say two weeks then one week).

QUALITY: The number of change requests at each iteration should decrease exponentially. The time to implement changes should also decrease, but not at the same rate because there is an overhead to making any change which is not proportional to the scale of the changes necessary.

NOTES: The skills needed for iterative development are different from those needed for formal build. Firstly the tools are different. Iterative build will be almost all done with CASE tools support, whereas formal build will probably involve procedural specification in some language, possibly a 3GL, possibly a generated pseudo-3GL or possibly a 4GL. However, the more important difference is that iterative development is based on user feedback to a suggested solution. The process is entirely driven by human interaction with a user who will not be 'technical' and may well not be familiar with the jargon of systems development. This is in contrast to a traditional build where the communication is by paper or electronic specification, backed up with discussion with systems analysts. The most likely profile for a fast-track iterative developer is a business-oriented analyst with CASE tools knowledge. Technically oriented developers must learn the CASE tools and then must acquire business knowledge and practise their interpersonal skills in an area where they have not been exercised before.

See "Redefining Systems Development Roles" on page 8.

Deliverables

PREREQUISITES

– physical database

(per partition)

– design prototype

– design specification

- schema definition

- systems facilities model

- menu definitions

- invocations of facilities from other facilities

– outstanding change requests to design specification

DELIVERABLES

– revised database definition

(per partition)

– implementable code
  (source plus executable or interpretable code)

– test data and plan

– online user documentation
  (help, hints, exception handling)

– revised design specification
  (reflecting changes made during development)

– outstanding change requests to design specification
  (partition and shared data changes)

TECHNIQUES: Iterative development is very attractive because it encourages ownership of the system by the stakeholders, because it can start to produce tangible results very quickly, and because the user-driven approach means that the delivered system is much more in line with what the end users need. Iterative development does not need a CASE tool, but without CASE tool support there are a number of risks and problems. Firstly, it becomes more difficult to make changes the more iterations we go through, because the code needs to be revised, then revised, then revised; either that or rewritten each time, which will destroy the productivity required. Secondly, this constantly revised code becomes less well structured and hence inefficient. Thirdly, and inevitably, the code becomes undocumented and undocumentable. The code itself is 'spaghetti' and the design documentation either non-existent or out of date.

If customization of the generated code is necessary, it should be delayed to the last iteration if possible, to minimize the management of combined generated and custom code in a single module.

See "Managing Iterative Build Projects" on page 26, "" on page 65 and "Prototyping" on page 61.

TOOLS: Using the Oracle CASE tools' repository and generator technology, at each iteration only the design documentation is maintained. The code is rebuilt each time round. This means that the documentation is up to date, the code is correctly structured for the job it is doing, and there is no loss of productivity at each iteration. Code customization is done with the Oracle Forms and Oracle Reports development tools. The CASE Reverse Engineering Utilities then create documentation of the changes.

Tasks

TASK 4

*Review system
components with users*

SUB-STAGE

*Iterate Build and
User Review*

DESCRIPTION

This task provides the developers and stakeholders with the opportunity to identify the details necessary to make the difference between a theoretically appropriate system and a usable and genuinely acceptable solution. As a side effect, it provides early training for users and, if successful, will leave the stakeholders with a sense of ownership of the system. The build iteration review is the most important task of the build stage.

Steps

1. Arrange review and brief participants.

2. Prepare test cases.

3. Conduct build iteration walkthrough.

4. Document, feed back and possibly implement requested changes.

5. Identify sources of further valid test data.

6. Agree status of system components.

ESTIMATING: The initial design prototype walkthrough will probably have taken a day. Build iteration reviews should take half a day or less, depending on the volume of changes. There will still be an overhead in arranging the meeting.

QUALITY: Quality assurance of Task 3 and Task 4 are really interdependent. The cycle time should diminish, the number of changes should diminish, the review time should diminish and the outstanding changes should relate increasingly to low priority aspects of the requirements.

NOTES: User review in the build stage is essentially the same as in the design prototype.

The review may identify changes to data definitions. These may be local, if they are to data that is private to the partition, or if they relate only to usage of the data within the specific partition. They may be external changes, if they relate to shared data definitions and might affect other partitions. External changes should not be made without analysing the impact on other partitions and consulting with other team members.

See "Managing Iterative Build Projects" on page 26, Task 10 in Chapter 5 and Task 5 on page 140.

Deliverables

PREREQUISITES

– schema definition

– implementable code

– test data and plan

– online user documentation

– module design specifications

– change requests to design specifications

DELIVERABLES

– revised

   • implementable code

   • test data and plan

   • online user documentation

   • design specification

– further change requests to design specification

– change requests to shared schema definition

– revised partition-specific schema definition

– revised partition-specific physical database

TECHNIQUES: The team should pay particular attention to the definition of the data and the business rules implemented in its structure because these may affect other partitions and will hence be more expensive to fix.

Reviewers should be encouraged to ask themselves such questions as *"Is this necessary?"*, *"Will this work in practice?"*, *"Will it cope with the vast majority of cases?"*, *"Can we deal with what it won't handle some other way?"*.

See "Prototype and Build Iteration Reviews" on page 66.

TOOLS: Changes requested can be documented directly as changes to module or data specifications in the Oracle CASE Dictionary, or using the free-text management facilities in the Oracle CASE Dictionary. Changes documented as text will then need to be transformed into modifications to the specifications of modules and data definitions, but it may be useful to capture the stakeholder's own statement of the problem and if a change may have an impact on other partitions, the exact nature of the change to be made may need to be discussed with other members of the team before we can decide exactly how it will be implemented. Use text to annotate the change requests if they affect shared data, not otherwise.

The Oracle CASE Dictionary also provides facilities to record change histories of modules in a more formal way. This is purely documentary. Many fast-track practitioners do not record module changes as module history as well. The issue is why you would want that documentation; in most cases it will be to resolve a dispute later. In a fast-track project we proceed on trust and cooperation between developer and user, not on a pseudo-contractual specification document. For this reason, module history is usually not maintained during fast-track development. It is still useful during maintenance, where looking back at the history to see why a module came to behave the way it does can be helpful in deciding how best to make a newly required change.

TASK 5

Collate external changes

DESCRIPTION

In reviews, changes requested to one partition can affect others. This task requires all the developers of all the partitions to get together and identify what actions are needed to accommodate the changes made in each other's partitions.

Steps

1. Identify changes to look and feel guidelines, resolve clashes and document.

2. Identify changes to data definitions, appearance and behaviour, resolve clashes and document.

3. Identify additions and changes to system architecture structure and document.

4. Identify changes and additions to each module's appearance and processing and document.

SUB-STAGE

*Iterate Build and
User Review*

ESTIMATING: This should be no more than a half-day session for the team.

QUALITY: As in many tasks, problems encountered here may well relate to unidentified issues that arose earlier. The number of external changes should be relatively low, since most major clashes should have been identified in the design prototype review. If that is not the case, re-examine how user reviews are done in general.

NOTES: This task may involve the project coordinator. External changes may contradict what the reviewing user (stakeholder) has requested. The project coordinator must resolve any such clashes. It is essential for everyone to remember that the objective of the project is to deliver benefit in the shortest possible time. Lengthy debates about small details can be very counter-productive. Seek to identify a compromise that can be implemented quickly. If no such compromise is apparent, try to isolate the impact so that the project can proceed whilst this issue is taken 'off line'. If necessary, redefine the scope of partitions to exclude the controversial element and identify a separate development to add it in later – in a later project? Most 'scope creep' occurs because people lose sight of the overall goal and concentrate too hard on small issues.

Deliverables

PREREQUISITES	DELIVERABLES

PREREQUISITES

– schema definition

– look and feel guidelines

– for each partition

  • implementable code

  • test data and plan

  • online user documentation

  • design specification

– change requests to design specification (all partitions)

DELIVERABLES

– schema definition change requests

– look and feel guidelines change requests

– change requests to design specification (all partitions)

– issues for user resolution

TECHNIQUES: It is inevitable that changes will affect a wider scope than the partition in which the change is requested. These changes will usually relate to database design, invariants or look and feel defaults for appearance and behaviour. Whenever possible they should be traced and resolved as soon as possible, during the build iteration. However, it is sensible for all the developers to get together in a single session after each build iteration to review all such changes, whether or not they are still unresolved. If nothing else, it helps keep the team in touch and aware of each other's concerns.

See "Prototype and Build Iteration Reviews" on page 66 and Task 11 in Chapter 5.

TOOLS: The Matrix Diagrammer can indicate which data is used by which modules and which business units. This information is the basis of impact analysis. It does not, however, resolve the problems, which remain for the team and project coordinator.

Tasks

TASK 6
Implement external changes

DESCRIPTION
This task implements the changes identified in the previous task.

Steps

1. Implement data definition, appearance and behaviour definition changes.

2. Implement look and feel guideline changes.

3. Create or revise prototypes to demonstrate change, if necessary.

SUB-STAGE
*Iterate Build and
User Review*

4. Review changes with project coordinator, if necessary.

5. Notify developers responsible for all affected modules that changed definitions are available.

ESTIMATING: The effort will probably not exceed a day unless it is necessary to review changes with the project coordinator. This may then take another half day and cause the elapsed time to increase. In many cases the collation and implementation of external changes will take place in a single session, which may then take a day (see previous task).

QUALITY: The project coordinator can assess the correctness of the changes, but if the changes are slight, it is probably not worth the time to review with the project coordinator. This is a risk/time trade-off.

NOTES: One class of change is to a module in another partition, which may be implementing the system architecture structure, and the other is to an underlying reusable component, normally a database design definition or look and feel guideline. The first kind will be the responsibility of the individual developers and will normally be integrated into the changes they are making in the next iteration anyway. The second kind may impact any and all of the partitions equally and may well be handled by one particular developer who has responsibility for data administration and database administration.

Deliverables

PREREQUISITES

– schema definition

– for each partition

- implementable code

- test data and plan

- online user documentation

- design specification

– change requests to design specification

DELIVERABLES

– revised implementable code

– revised test data and plan

– revised online user documentation

– revised design specification

– revised schema definition

– revised physical database

– outstanding change requests

TECHNIQUES: External changes that need to be implemented before the next build iteration can start include those that the user project coordinator needs to review before they can be adopted by all the developers, for example look and feel guidelines changes, and those that are a dependency for the next build iteration, such as database definition changes.

TOOLS: All changes can and should be documented in the Oracle CASE Dictionary. Database schema changes can then be implemented by the Data Definition Language (DDL) generator and look and feel guidelines will be enforced in all **future** application code generation. If test data already exists, some data definition changes may not be fully automated. Also, look and feel guidelines are not enforced retrospectively: any code generated previously will not reflect the new guidelines unless it is generated again.

Tasks

TASK 7
Prepare test plans and data

DESCRIPTION

This task prepares for testing in the traditional approach to unit test and build.

Steps

1. Review requirements specification.
2. Prepare test plan.
3. Prepare test data.

SUB-STAGE
Conduct Formal Build

4. Prepare milestone plan.
5. Arrange quality checks.
6. Review plans.

ESTIMATING: This should take no more than one day for an experienced implementor for a single module, but may be extended if testing requires large volumes or complex data.

QUALITY: Check deliverables to house standards. The project manager should briefly review all test plans. The milestones should relate to the completion of stages in the development. These will be code completion and test completion. Code milestones should reflect the priorities (MoSCoW model) and may be further split into basic functionality, complex processing, special-case handling and user interface. This provides a simpler testing environment. The basic functionality is implemented before we add the complexities, which means that if anything has to be traded out it will be lower priority.

NOTES: Formal build elements of a fast-track project will normally be the responsibility of implementation specialists. Hence there may be an additional need for interpretation and amplification of the requirements by the team members who have been involved from the beginning of the project.

Although the plans created here may be revised significantly during the development, it is still worth having them.

For some modules it may not make sense to develop stand-alone test plans. They may only be accessed as part of a multi-step transaction. In this case the test plan may correspond to the whole transaction.

The test plans will almost certainly not be complete at this stage. Create standard case and boundary test data at this stage and evolve it and add to it during the code and test cycle. If the database design might change during the development in a way that cannot be managed without re-creating the database tables, consider creating scripts to unload and load data. With modification at each revision, these can then be used to re-create test data after database definition changes.

Deliverables

PREREQUISITES	DELIVERABLES

PREREQUISITES

– schema definition

– design prototype

– design specification

DELIVERABLES

– for each module

- test plan

- test data

- milestone plan

TECHNIQUES: The Formal Build Sub-stage should be split into separate tasks in order to provide milestones for project control. This is not specifically a fast-track approach, but because time is of the essence, tight control on the use of time is even more important. Having frequent milestones does not help you to use time better, but it tells you sooner if there is a problem.

The milestone plan will indicate the expected completion dates for each task in the Formal Build Sub-stage, including milestones for code development and test. The default milestone plan would look something like the following:

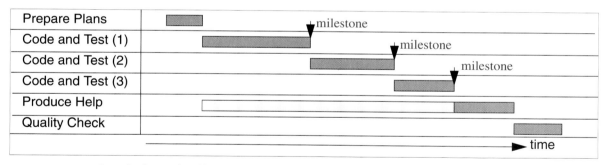

where the first code milestone would represent the structure and data manipulation, the second milestone would represent the remaining 'Must have' requirements and the third represents the 'Should have' functionality. If progress is better than expected then 'Could have' functionality can be added in during the third milestone. Often 'Could have' functionality is just a more attractive implementation of part of the 'Must have' functionality, probably planned for the second milestone. With this approach we can get a clear indication of whether we will have time for extra functionality relatively early in the development.

See "Managing Formal Build Projects" on page 25 and "Test Planning and Testing" on page 33.

TOOLS: The test plan will normally be an Oracle CASE Dictionary document. Test data will normally reside in a test database.

TASK 8
Develop and test a code milestone

DESCRIPTION

This task produces a stable testable unit of code.

Steps

1. Develop next code milestone.

2. Unit test and correct (code, test plan, test data).

3. Review and challenge specification, if necessary.

SUB-STAGE
Conduct Formal Build

4. Review plans if necessary.

5. Replace stub module in the module network.

6. Generate the menu structure to exclude stub and include real modules.

ESTIMATING: The duration of a coding milestone (and the number of milestones necessary to complete a particular development) is dependent on the experience of the developer. More milestones mean more management time and overhead activities. Fewer mean less control and a weaker framework. On a fast-track project, the implementation specialists are unlikely to need a high level of support.

QUALITY: Test plans and results together with adherence to milestones provide the quality and process control mechanisms.

NOTES: The use of milestones provides a good mechanism for timebox management of the process, but is justified in non-timeboxed code development as it provides a strong framework for less experienced developers and a good mechanism for monitoring project progress.

Second and subsequent milestones may be the addition of complexity or additional functionality to a previous coding milestone. This is sometimes known as step-wise refinement. Or a milestone may implement the next stage of processing, based on the outputs of the previous milestone. This is partitioning at a lower level, sometimes known as modularization. Milestones should be defined in whatever way is necessary to match priorities and to fit in with the scale and style of the development.

Steps 5 and 6 will apply if a module under development replaces a stub module that was created for the design prototype. Only replace the stub after module development is complete, prior to integration testing.

Deliverables

PREREQUISITES

– schema definition

– design prototype **or**

– implementable code
  (from previous code milestone)

– design specification

– design and code change requests
  (from previous code milestone)

– test plan

– test data

DELIVERABLES

– revised schema definition

– revised design prototype

– revised design specification

– revised test plan

– revised test data

– implementable code

TECHNIQUES: This is not a book on programming and program design: there are many texts already written on that subject advocating different approaches. Whatever techniques are used for design, the critical success factors are that they are well understood, properly followed, based on sound principles and backed by pragmatic experience. Here we are concerned with how we develop complex procedural programs within fast-track projects.

See "Managing Formal Build Projects" on page 25 and Task 7.

TOOLS: The choice of implementation language will affect the degree to which the Oracle CASE tools can assist and hence the degree to which the CASE tools will drive the process. The essence of fast-track is that we exploit the available tools to achieve our objectives as quickly and easily as possible. This means that if our tool set supports one approach better than another, we will favour that approach. Using PL/SQL to define procedures in the Oracle CASE Dictionary means that these procedures can be generated as ORACLE database procedures and then reused, either nested into procedure packages, invoked from triggers on database events or invoked from Oracle Forms on user interface events. An alternative approach is to use the Oracle CASE Dictionary only to document the existence of the procedures, and then to develop them independently in C, for example.

TASK 9
Collate external changes

DESCRIPTION
This task is identical to Task 5.

All partitions will need to identify the impact of external changes necessary as a result of user reviews. If possible this should be at the end of a code milestone, if this can be synchronized with the iterative partitions. In any event, external changes can affect formal build partitions.

SUB-STAGE
Conduct Formal Build

Steps

1. Identify changes to look and feel guidelines, resolve clashes and document.

2. Identify changes to database design definitions, appearance and behaviour, resolve clashes and document.

3. Identify additions and changes to system architecture structure and document.

4. Identify changes and additions to each module's appearance and processing and document.

ESTIMATING: This should be a half day session for the team.

QUALITY: As in many tasks, problems encountered here may well relate to unidentified issues that arose earlier. The number of external changes should be relatively low, since most major clashes should have been identified in the design prototype review. If that is not the case, re-examine how user reviews are done in general.

NOTES: Formal build partitions are likely to be concerned with implementing background processing. This will mean that data definition changes are the ones most likely to affect a formal build partition. Look and feel and data appearance and behaviour defaults are less likely to have any effect.

See Task 5 above.

Deliverables

PREREQUISITES

– database definition

– look and feel guidelines

– for each partition

  • implementable code

  • test data and plan

  • online user documentation

  • design specification

– change requests to design specification
  (all partitions)

DELIVERABLES

– database definition change requests

– look and feel guidelines change requests

– for all partitions

  • change requests to design specification

– issues for user resolution

TECHNIQUES: See Task 5 above.

TOOLS:　　　See Task 5 above.

TASK 10
Implement external changes

DESCRIPTION

This task is identical to Task 6.

Steps

1. Implement data definition, appearance and behaviour defaults changes.

2. Implement look and feel guideline changes.

3. Create prototypes to demonstrate change, if necessary.

SUB-STAGE
Conduct Formal Build

4. Review changes with project coordinator, if necessary.

5. Notify developers responsible for all affected modules that changed definitions are available.

ESTIMATING: The effort will probably not exceed a day unless it is necessary to review changes with the project coordinator.

QUALITY: The project coordinator can assess the correctness of the changes, but if the changes are slight, it is probably not worth the time to review with the project coordinator. This is a risk/time trade-off.

NOTES: Data definition changes may impact any and all of the partitions equally and may well be handled by one particular developer who has responsibility for data administration and database administration. However, since data definition changes are the ones most likely to be of interest to the developer of a formal build partition, then she or he is the most likely candidate for data administrator.

See Task 6 above.

Deliverables

PREREQUISITES

– schema definition

– for each partition

- implementable code

- test data and plan

- online user documentation

- design specification

– change requests to design specification
(all partitions)

DELIVERABLES

– revised implementable code

– revised test data and plan

– revised online user documentation

– revised design specification

– outstanding change requests

TECHNIQUES: See Task 6 above.

NOTES: See Task 6 above.

Tasks

TASK 11
Produce online help etc.

DESCRIPTION

The online help forms the bulk of the user documentation of a fast-track project. Production of online help is often not recognized as part of unit build and test: it should be, and is for a fast-track project.

Steps

1. Review module(s) that implement the facility the users require.

SUB-STAGE
Conduct Formal Build

2. Identify necessary documentation to explain the need for the facility.

3. Identify necessary documentation for operation of the facility.

4. Identify necessary documentation to explain exception processing and provide guidance in exception recovery.

5. Create text to meet these needs.

6. Implement text as help at appropriate interface points.

7. Review all help material in context.

ESTIMATING: For a single module the user help should not take more than one day to develop. Users should contribute to the writing and the developers concentrate on structuring the help and making it accessible at the appropriate point in the operation.

QUALITY: The users are the only valid arbiters. If they are involved in the process the results are more likely to be acceptable.

NOTES: Just as in the development of the system facilities, the development of online help, error messages and user hint messages can best be developed with user participation. The different classifications of messages (identifying business process supported, providing operational assistance and dealing with exceptions) should be separated and associated with the appropriate parts of the user dialogue. All this is common to the development of user help in iterative build. However, the process is likely to be different in formal build because there will not necessarily have been user input at each milestone which can contribute to the evolution of the help material in parallel with the system functionality.

Deliverables

PREREQUISITES

– schema definition

– design specification

– implementable code

– test data and plan

DELIVERABLES

– user documentation
  (help, hints, exception handling)

TECHNIQUES: Always use the terminology that the end users themselves would use. Requirements statements from the users and questions or comments made by users at reviews provide the most important source. Users should, however, review **all** the help material on the screen in context.

TOOLS: In the Oracle CASE tools help and hint messages associated with the module, table and column definitions can be made available for reuse by any module accessing that data. Context-specific help can be entered for each use of a column or table by a module if required. If there is a network of modules calling modules of which only the initial module is accessible directly by the user, then the help material for all the modules should be associated with the one module that the end user can see. From a user viewpoint, the facility only has one invocation, so it is, from the user viewpoint, a single module.

Even if modules are not invoked from the user interface, information about them can still be made accessible to the user by means of help material for menu items that do nothing when invoked except provide an explanation of what the facility does and how it is invoked, possibly by a time event, possibly as part of regular operations (for example, data load from another system).

It is also possible to include multimedia in the online help using Oracle Book or other tools.

Tasks

TASK 12

Quality check code and testing process

DESCRIPTION

This task ensures the code quality of formal build modules.

Steps

1. Ensure that hand-coded facilities have the same level of reliability as generated code.

2. Check code for adherence to standards.

SUB-STAGE

Conduct Formal Build

3. Check test plans and results.

4. Fix and retest changes requested (last time only).

ESTIMATING: The objective of quality check is not to examine each line of code to see if the checker would have done it that way. Quality check is a brief process to ensure that the procedures have been followed. However, it must include time to correct any omissions: there is no point testing if there is no time to correct (see notes below).

QUALITY: If quality checking is not being effective, we will see excessive errors in implemented code. Such errors are a failure of the quality process, which is designed to find them, rather than a failure of the development process, which cannot avoid introducing them occasionally.

NOTES: Quality checking is an explicit task in formal build – generated code automatically adheres to the look and feel guidelines and other development standards, hand-developed code does not. Also generated code does not need to be tested, only the design, and this is tested by user review. Hand-coded facilities need to be tested to ensure that the requirements have been correctly implemented.

For generated code, test results should be user reviewed. Where the coding process is not automatic the testing must be more exhaustive, particularly boundary conditions in data and destructive user testing. Quality checking should be concerned that these types of test have been planned and conducted.

For all but the final code milestone, fixes can be left for the next milestone, in the form of change requests. The final quality-checking task should allow time for immediate fixes and retest if necessary.

Deliverables

PREREQUISITES

– schema definition

– design prototype

– design specification

– test plan

– test data

– milestone plan

DELIVERABLES

– design and code change requests

– design and code changes
  (last time only)

– plan changes

TECHNIQUES: The most effective quality check approach for code is inspection of the code, plans and specifications. Quality checking should not just find bugs in the code as developed, it should seek out bugs in the process whereby the code was developed, so that the process can be improved next time. It is true that the number of bugs is a fair indicator of the quality of the process, but it is not the only one, and we have all known developers in our professional lives who could, in very short timescales, produce wonderful functionality, which was not quite the functionality that the user asked for or the specification demanded and which could never be maintained, even by the person who wrote it. Organizations and their environments change, never more rapidly than now, so a good system must be able to change with them, or cease to be a good system. Many bad systems need no maintenance; they are just ignored, never get used and so never need to change.

A successful fast-track development, just like any other, will need to change after implementation, so maintainability is still not something we can discard. However, see also "One-shot Fast-track" on page 170.

See "Test Planning and Testing" on page 33.

TOOLS: The Oracle CASE tools, using the Matrix Diagrammer, Impact Analysis Reports and Reverse Engineering Facilities, can present the quality inspector with the information required and can automate some parts of the comparison of code to specification. The Oracle Forms and Oracle Reports development tools themselves provide facilities for code inspection; Oracle Browser and Oracle Data Query provide access and analysis of the test data.

Tasks

TASK 13
Prepare for integration test

DESCRIPTION

This task prepares the data and plan for the integration test, based on the unit test data and plans of the developers of each partition.

Steps

1. Load static data.

2. Identify integration test objectives and prepare test scenarios to achieve them.

3. Identify, assign and brief tester, user and developer.

ESTIMATING: Approximately three to five days effort will be needed in parallel to development activity, reusing unit test scripts. All team members will contribute some time.

QUALITY: Check that all partition interoperation (data or facility) is covered by a test scenario and all unit test scenarios are included.

NOTES: If possible, develop the integration scenarios early in the stage. In this way the unit test data can be developed to fit together and be reused in integration test preparation. Even so, time will be spent in integrating unit tests into appropriate scenarios, because integration testing is not intended to repeat testing that is part of the development process. It is intended to establish that the system works as a whole, in a way that is consistent with what the users expect. To this end the integration test scenarios should be developed to cover:

- external changes that have been identified in the development
- instances of shared data (created in one partition and used elsewhere)
- instances of navigation from facilities in one partition to another
- instances of the same user group having access to more than one partition
- realistic volumes and loadings.

Testers should be the users who reviewed the developing system. There can be an advantage in introducing additional new users at integration testing to expand the knowledge of the new system in the user population and make training easier. There is a risk that they will not accept the system as their colleagues have specified it. If this happens it can jeopardize the whole project and would hence seem to be something to be avoided. However, if the system is not right, then it is better to know earlier than later. There should be at least one user to cover each partition and all should have knowledge of interoperation with the business areas represented by the other partitions.

Deliverables

PREREQUISITES

– test plans

– test data

– design specifications

DELIVERABLES

– integration test plan

– integration test data

TECHNIQUES: Preparing for the integration test is often almost invisible as a separate task. Provided the developers bear in mind the need to reuse their test scenarios for integration testing, and they use common base data for all testing, then integration test preparation will require little more than re-editing the scripts to create scenarios that span multiple modules, passing control and data between the modules as will be required in live operation. Integration testing is not concerned with detailed exception and data testing, since these would only repeat tests already successfully completed in unit testing. Integration testing ensures that:

- data entered in modules of one partition is as expected by modules of other partitions that use that data

- other links (for example, reports developed in one partition being also invokable from a menu in another partition) work as required

- there is consistency of look and feel throughout.

See "Test Planning and Testing" on page 33, "Preparing for the Review" on page 66 and Task 2 in Chapter 5.

TOOLS: Where the CASE generators have been used, based on a style guide defined by a look and feel prototype, consistency of look and feel should not be a significant problem. There will be exceptions, where user requirements have legitimately overridden the rules. Other users should get the opportunity to review such decisions in integration test scenarios.

In a large formal project where configuration management and project coordination are likely to be significant issues, test scenarios and data set-up scripts may well be managed as Oracle CASE Dictionary documents and modules respectively. In a fast-track project, the level of administrative overhead would probably outweigh the benefits, since the team will be small, experienced and motivated.

TASK 14

Conduct integration test

DESCRIPTION

This task ensures that all the individual facilities of the system interoperate as expected and required.

Steps

1. Work through each test scenario.

2. Document all errors and unexpected results as change requests.

SUB-STAGE

Integrate Components

3. Review change requests with users.

ESTIMATING: Allow two days elapsed time, with the whole team assigned plus user representatives.

QUALITY: Ensure that all scenarios are covered. Anything more than a single-figure percentage of change requests relating to unimplemented functionality implies that the scope of the project may be creeping. This can only be managed if the plans are adjusted to allow for additional work and the replan is approved by sponsor and stakeholders.

NOTES: The testing time should be timeboxed. If it finishes inside the time, the saved time can be used to implement and retest change requests. These will normally only be low priority, apart from a small number of genuine 'bugs'.

The users should get the opportunity to discuss any changes that are not just bug fixes. These can arise because of a misunderstanding about the original requirement. If we can misunderstand it once, we can do it twice, so take extra care to get it right this time.

There may be a tendency for user opinion to 'flip-flop' between equivalent alternative solutions. Be aware of it and resist it. Use the sponsor or project coordinator to arbitrate.

Deliverables

PREREQUISITES

– integration test plan

– integration test data

– schema definition

– design specification

– implementable code

– user documentation

– outstanding change requests

DELIVERABLES

– integration test results

  • test coverage

  • comment

  • status (tested ok/tested, needs rework)

TECHNIQUES: Integration testing is essentially the same as user review. In integration testing, by its very nature, all the partitions will be tested together. This will make the management of the test more complex, since all the developers and users will be involved. Provided the test scenarios and other review documentation have been prepared, this should not increase complexity and risk.

See Task 4, "Test Planning and Testing" on page 33 and "Prototype and Build Iteration Reviews" on page 66.

TOOLS: All change requests should be logged at the time they occur and classified (bug or enhancement) and assigned an initial priority by the user. These priorities may be revised later (see next task), but it is necessary to capture the initial expectation. Change requests can be recorded as module history events in Oracle CASE Dictionary, as free-text notes associated with modules and data definitions or as documents associated with modules, and data definitions, or as part of a structure of test results documents that are cross-referenced through the Matrix Diagrammer to the system components (modules, tables, etc.) that they affect. The advantage of this last approach, as suggested for test scenarios, is that developers and managers can see the 'big picture' easily, and identify which modules have outstanding change requests and which tests have been conducted.

Tasks

TASK 15
*Review test results
and rework*

DESCRIPTION

This task implements outstanding change requests. When these have been implemented we need to retest, which of course leads to more changes...

Steps

1. Classify all change requests by priority.

2. Implement changes by priority.

SUB-STAGE
Integrate Components

3. Update user documentation.

4. Update design specification.

5. Identify and make any necessary changes to test scenarios.

ESTIMATING: Allow three days' elapsed time, for the whole team assigned plus the user sponsor to assign priorities.

QUALITY: There should be test results for all scenarios, identifying the changes necessary. Each change should be dealt with by this task.

NOTES: Timebox the fixing time and use the Must have/Should have/Could have/Won't have (MoSCoW) model to prioritize work. The priorities may be user assigned, but generally they will be inherited from the priority of the facilities of which they are part.

Some of the change requests may have arisen because the original test scenarios did not demonstrate the operation of the system fully or properly. Sometimes the response to a change request is to add a step to the test scenario to demonstrate more effectively the system functionality that was thought to be missing.

Some of the change requests may have arisen for performance reasons. This is not often a problem in development, but integration testing may identify the need for system performance tuning. In a fast-track project this is usually satisfied by the design and implementation of appropriate database design tuning, including indexing, and possibly minimal denormalization.

Deliverables

PREREQUISITES

– integration test results

– design specification
  (including priorities)

DELIVERABLES

– revised integration test plan

– revised integration test data

– revised database schema definition

– revised physical database

– revised design specification

– revised implementable code

– revised user documentation

– outstanding change requests

TECHNIQUES: Integration test rework is a microcosm of a build iteration, so the same approach applies. In addition, there may need to be a review of priorities, to drive the rework via a timebox.

This task should create the code to implement each change, the documentation changes to reflect any new behaviour and, if necessary, revisions to the test plans to cover the revised functionality. Any low priority changes which are excluded because of lack of time should be identified as such to the users and the test scenarios revised to indicate expected behaviour in the results and notes.

See Task 3, Task 7, Task 8, Task 11, "Reviewing Priorities" on page 69 and "Test Planning and Testing" on page 33.

TOOLS: The tools used in building, documenting and preparing to test the system components will be needed again here.

Tasks

TASK 16
Conduct integration retest

DESCRIPTION
This task repeats Task 14 if necessary.

Steps

1. Rerun integration test scenarios.

2. Document and prioritize any remaining change requests.

3. Fix necessary bugs.

SUB-STAGE
Integrate Components

4. Review test results; if necessary, repeat Task 15 and Task 16.

ESTIMATING: Retest should take less time than the initial test, perhaps one day, plus one day final fix and review. The whole team will be assigned plus user representatives.

QUALITY: There should be no change requests in retest which remain from the initial test. Retest should reveal only a low percentage of the number of original change requests. Consider this as your last opportunity to get it right; there should be no loose ends now.

NOTES: After the retest, there will inevitably be some new changes generated. The project manager and user sponsor must review these and take a decision on whether to repeat the test and fix cycle. Some time may well be necessary to fix any new bugs which have been introduced.

Deliverables

PREREQUISITES

– integration test plan

– integration test data

– schema definition

– design specification

– implementable code

– user documentation

– outstanding change requests

DELIVERABLES

– integration test results

- test coverage

- comment

- status (tested ok/tested, needs rework)

TECHNIQUES: See Task 14.

TOOLS: See Task 14.

Summary

The completion of the Build Stage is undeniably the high spot of an information systems development project, especially in fast-track, where continuous user participation means that the system is already accepted by at least some of the user population. The difficulty that sometimes arises at this point is a sense of anticlimax, a sense that the hard part of the job is over. Full implementation may well only be a formality, but there may still be user training, data take-on, performance trials and other transition tasks to complete, in which case the end of the build stage is not the time to start relaxing. The major deliverables of the project are now in place, and there is no doubt time for a little self-congratulation. But the project manager needs to be very aware that like a mountaineering team at the peak, there is much to be done before the job is complete. A careless step on the descent can be just as fatal as on the ascent, so concentration is just as important.

During build, the stage end must be viewed as just another, although very important, milestone, not as the end of the hard work. Provided this is remembered, then it is true to say that **most** of the hard work is done by the end of the build stage. Maybe this is the opportunity for a **modest** celebration, before we tackle the last stage.

7

COMPLETING THE LIFE-CYCLE

Transition

The transition stage is when the new system moves from the development environment and goes to work in the business. There are a number of jobs still to be done after build and test is complete before we can 'throw the switch'. Figure 7-1 on page 166 shows the main transition tasks in a formal development. The same objectives have to be achieved in a fast-track project, so the tasks are essentially the same but the mechanisms employed are different.

User Training and Acceptance Testing

Because of the way in which a fast-track development will have been conducted, the requirement for user training will be significantly lower. Many, if not all, of the users will have experience of the system from user reviews and integration testing. There may be no need to conduct any more formal training before production. Even if more training is needed, it should be the responsibility of the users themselves. They will be more than capable by now, having worked with the system extensively and written the user documentation. Only in the preparation and planning of the training events themselves might there be a need for input from the development team, and that may well come from an internal training department in the business. Likewise the acceptance test is really a rerun of integration testing and will therefore only be required if there have been significant changes in the environment or if other acceptance trials have been necessary, for example, performance tuning (see "Performance Trials" on page 167).

Data Migration

Many fast-track projects will be 'green-field' developments, where no existing data is needed from legacy systems, and others will add new functionality to existing databases. In both these cases no data migration

Figure 7-1
The Transition Stage Dependencies

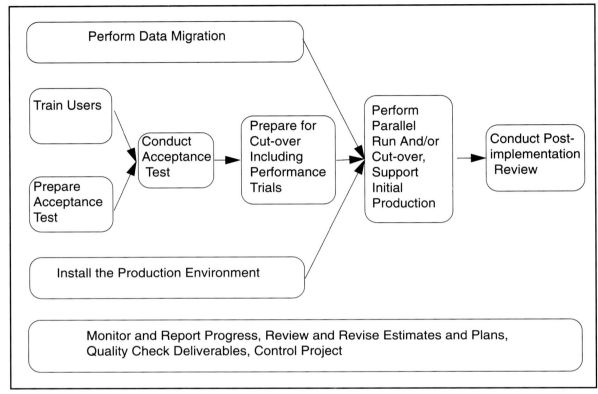

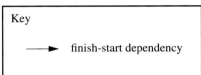

Key

finish-start dependency

will be required. Some fast-track projects will need to load production data from an existing non-relational system. The reason for choosing fast-track may have been that development on the existing platform is too slow to respond to user needs, so the requirement is to move data to a different platform and build the new functionality rapidly to process it. However, an evolutionary approach is not the best approach to a batch system-to-system interface, which needs to map data structures from one database onto the corresponding structures of the new one. Any database changes in the target system, which means nearly every external change that emerges from the build, will impact the interface. An interface of this kind should not be developed as just another synchronized project partition in the project because, although the external change management mechanisms defined in the Build Stage will handle the requirement, the fact that all database definition changes will have an impact means that we will probably do an unacceptable amount of rework. It is better if the interface is defined as a separate build stage, running slightly behind the main development, so that it will not start until the rest of the development has been integrated and the number of database changes will be very low. If database stability is not an issue, for example, where the project is redeveloping a well-understood requirement, then the interface development may run just one iteration behind the rest of the development. Figure 7-2 shows how the project plan can take advantage of early stability in the database design.

Figure 7-2

Fast-track Developments with Batch Interfacing

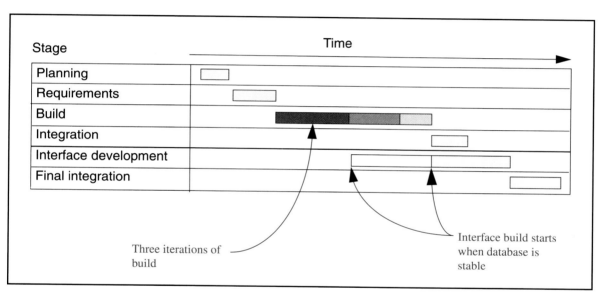

A data migration utility can be regarded as a one-off batch interface. When the database structure for the new system is mature, as indicated in Figure 7-2, the mapping for unloading and loading the data is known and the loader software can be built. By transition, the data migration software should be ready, and migration can be performed in the normal manner, with the proviso that subsequent performance tuning may modify the database structure and require modification and re-execution of data migration.

Performance Trials

A fast-track project will normally be based on the premise that a normalized database design will provide more than adequate performance to support the application. As performance improvements in hardware and software occur all the time this will become true for more and more requirements. Any application with critical and difficult-to-meet performance criteria may not be amenable to a pure fast-track approach. In such cases it may be wise to separate development from tuning, which then becomes a discrete activity during transition.

Environment Installation, Cut-over and Production Support

These activities may have all the characteristics of a standard project; however, it is likely that they will present fewer problems because of the scale, and because of the level of user participation and 'ownership' that generally characterize fast-track projects.

Post-implementation Review

It is good practice to review any project after completion. What did we do well? What did we do badly? There is always an opportunity to reflect what we have learned as input to the next project. The concept of reusing a successful project plan as the basis of the next one is sometimes known as templating. In essence, Chapters 4 to 6 of this book represent a template for a fast-track project, but this template will be refined and tuned by every project that is based upon it. If we are using project management tools that can hold templates, we should seek to improve the template we use for each project or create a new template based on the current project to let others avoid the hard lessons we have learned. This will be particularly true when adopting a new approach, new tools and techniques such as fast-track. Just as a large part of the productivity in fast-track development comes from reusing components of the design, so too we should apply reusability to the project plans themselves.

Hyper Fast-track

Even in fast-track projects, there is still scope to slim the process down further. Where the requirement is very simple and we can impose additional constraints on the development, we can move even faster. The additional characteristics of hyper fast-track are listed below. Hyper fast-track is a good way to start: inexpensive, low risk, short pay-back time and with skill, confidence and experience gained on the way.

Hyper Fast-track Constraints

- No customization of screen and report layouts:

  - custom code costs effort and is almost always only cosmetic. The generators will automatically create layouts that conform to the look and feel of the project style guide.

- No batch updating utilities:

  - batch updates generally require the specification of procedural transformations, and these usually take longer to develop and require more testing.

- No more than two partitions:

  - the number of interfaces between two partitions is one, between two it is three, between four it is six. Complexity in communications within the team increases more than linearly with an increase in the number of partitions.

- No more than two stakeholders:

  - one per partition, with no second authority to consult and no possibility of conflicting interests bedevilling the development.

- No more than three developers:

  - one to own each partition and one to take up the slack in testing, integration and administration.

- No more than twelve weeks elapsed time:

  - this is an arbitrary limit, which represents the time from initial scoping meetings with the sponsor to the acceptance of the system by users. Twelve weeks is plenty of time for three developers to produce a useful system. Use the limit to focus the scope and simplify the project control. When your next project milestone is only days away at most, it is easier to keep control.

The constraints dictated above for hyper fast-track are somewhat arbitrary, and as an organization gains in experience these rules can be relaxed, little by little, until you are achieving twelve-week timescales for full life-cycle developments of considerable size and complexity. In addition to the gains that can be made from limiting the scope and complexity of the project, we can do more: we can exclude some tasks, and diminish the scale of others.

- No look and feel prototype:

  - Accept layouts according to existing or default style guides. This removes the need for a step in the requirements stage. Since the task is not, by default, on the critical path, there is only a gain to be had from excluding it if there is a shortage of user or developer resources.

- Only one build iteration:

  - After the design prototype, if it can be agreed that only the changes identified at that point, and of these possibly only the 'Must haves' are to be implemented, then the build stage can be reduced to one iteration.

- Only basic online user help documentation:

  - If users accept the responsibility for online documentation, then developers can document only specific behaviour and leave the rest for users to add as and when required. With the Oracle CASE tools this can be done anytime by means of a simple utility, without altering any code.

- Only design-level functional definitions:

  - By excluding documentation of the function model at the business process level, we are weakening our ability to subsequently evolve the system as the business changes and we are less well placed to understand how it should integrate into subsequent developments. If initial implementation is seen to be more important than subsequent maintenance, then why not?

The constraints of hyper fast-track concentrate on simplifying the requirements in order to raise the speed. Any fast-track development done in this way will still be documented and can still be integrated into other developments. The short cuts above go further. Projects run with these constraints will not necessarily be as flexible in the light of future changes in the business, but that may not be important in certain circumstances. These are the so-called 'one-shot fast-tracks'.

One-shot Fast-track

Sometimes an organization needs to respond to short-term tactical needs in the certain knowledge that the solutions will be disposable. There may be a transitional step between an old way of doing business and the new way which cannot be implemented yet. There may be a need to react quickly to an environmental change, for example, a new government reporting requirement; this will eventually be satisfied by a package system that is being acquired, but a stop-gap system needs to be produced for the interim period.

In these cases it is unnecessary to stick to the high standards for documentation, consistency of look and feel, and reusability of design.

We could have a one-shot fast-track project without the other characteristics of hyper fast-track. It may be bigger than two partitions, it may have more that two users, but if it is going to be replaced within twelve months or so, then regardless of the scope, there is little point in providing deliverables whose major value is in maintenance or reuse. It is important to recognize this at the scoping stage and to specifically exclude the unnecessary deliverables from the plan and be absolutely sure that the sponsor fully understands and accepts this, and, furthermore, that a dispassionate review of the business case indicates that this really is a short life-span system.

There are countless systems in maintenance today, extremely costly maintenance, that were always intended to be one shots. There are far fewer genuine one shots than you would expect. If you find that difficult to believe, look around your own installation. Do you have any antique one shots soaking up maintenance resource like a camel in an oasis? When was the last time you scrapped a system after twelve months because you had planned to, not because it never worked in the first place? Nonetheless, the one shot is a valid part of the developer's armoury, but it should not be overused. **And remember, even if it is a one-shot or hyper fast-track system it must still do what the organization needs it to do.**

Chapter

8

THE NEXT STEP

In this book we have looked at the whole life-cycle of fast-track projects, including the tasks, the techniques, the deliverables and the management, but this is no more than an intellectual exercise until it is put into practice. How can an organization do that?

Implementing Fast-track

CASE can be described simply as computerization for the Information Systems (IS) department. When we buy CASE tools we are buying a packaged system for the IS department just as we might buy an accounting package or a manufacturing package for other functions of the business. And as with any other package, the success of the implementation will rest on fitting the package to the organization, and in recognizing how to get the best out of the package and using it accordingly. This is nothing new to people who have implemented packaged computer systems, so we ought to be able to apply some of the lessons in implementing CASE.

CASE implementation highlights one of the problems of all package implementation. This is the problem of mismatch. If the package does not support the way we want to perform some process, what are we to do? The traditional approach in accounting and other packages has been to customize the package to fit the business process, an off-the-peg with alterations approach. The conventional approach of some CASE vendors has been to discard the business processes and replace them with a prescriptive methodology, a 'one size fits all' approach. Both these approaches have had successes and failures. To identify the real cause of success and failure we have to look not just at how well the tool fits the processes, or how well we can make the processes fit the tool, but at what are the appropriate processes, and then how we use tools to support those processes.

Applying this idea to real organizations is where fast-track came from. There are two main approaches to computer systems development that you meet in IS departments. In one, the emphasis is on a repeatable process, predictability, maintainability and risk reduction. In the other, the emphasis is on responsiveness and productivity. The shortcomings of each of these approaches are the strengths of the other, so they seem to be at odds with each other, probably because they reflect the cultures and self-images of the organizations in which they are applied.

Most of the major trends in application development technology represent attempts to increase productivity without increasing the risk or reduce risk without affecting productivity. The industry seems to embrace one new panacea after another in pursuit of increased productivity and/or lower risk:

- Fourth-generation programming languages (4GLs)

- Code Generators

- Integrated CASE (I-CASE)

- Object-oriented Programming Languages (OOPLs)

- Graphical User Interface Builders (GUI Builders).

Of course it is impossible to categorize individual products. They evolve from one category to another, more or less successfully. New categories and products appear, absorbing and extending the advantages of existing products and categories. The lesson must be that no single technology can represent an end-point. There must be continual change.

If fast-track is to succeed in delivering business-driven, end-user-oriented systems, rapidly and without sacrificing maintainability and repeatability, it will be in organizations that can be responsive to short-term needs whilst maintaining a cogent long-term vision. It is not just a matter of having the latest tools, it is also the way in which they are used. For many organizations this will involve change to the way things are currently done. But it is not a 'one size fits all' change. It will be an evolutionary change, exploiting current strengths and building new strengths. This evolution will be different for each organization.

For the informal organization, adoption of fast-track will be characterized by the introduction of more formal processes, but without stifling the flexibility that is an existing strength. The fast-track life-cycle encourages such organizations to develop more reusable and maintainable designs, through the early emphasis on style guides and enriched common data definitions. The fast-track management techniques help them to improve predictability and repeatability.

For formal organizations, adoption of fast-track will be characterized by the introduction of more flexible techniques and more automation, without sacrificing standards of documentation or maintainability. Workshops and evolutionary development provide a faster route to more user-acceptable systems. Oracle CASE tools provide a very high level of automation for the declarative approach to requirements definition. Some development organizations will adopt this approach in order to get sustainable productivity gains.

Making the Change

The first step is always a pilot project: not too large, but not trivially small, not business-mission critical, but not irrelevant. From this pilot we create a skills base from which to expand. We also begin to evolve the way we develop computer systems now towards the way we want to do it in the future. This is the most difficult part of the process for an organization to achieve – not the change of tools, nor the change of skills, but the change of culture. An organization that does not believe in the need for change, all the way up and down, will not succeed in changing itself. One of our favourite management texts, if only for the title, is *Teaching the Elephant to Dance* (Belasco, 1990). The book is all about creating an awareness of the need to change and empowering organizations to make changes. Information Systems departments that want to gain the benefits of fast-track development must really want that change, must really fear the cost of not changing. After that will come the hard work of implementing the change: from pilot project to skills transfer programmes, to adopting project templates and style guides, to building a broad base of expertise, and, having established the process, getting regular feedback and continually making improvements.

But without a recognition that change is necessary, real change will not come.

Establish the Need for Change

Indicators are:

- application backlog
- maintenance effort
- user satisfaction
- employee productivity
- employee satisfaction
- competitive strength – outsourcing
- business effectiveness – competitors' informations systems.

'If it ain't bust, don't fix it.' But how many of us can honestly say that our development approaches *'ain't bust'*? Even if we have few concerns about the first five items, the last two are particularly interesting.

In recent years an increasing number of organizations have set arbitrary productivity targets for their Information Systems departments. Where these targets are not met, an increasing number of Information Systems departments are finding themselves competing with outsourcing agencies, and being either replaced or migrated to the outsourcer. Many of these deals result in the same staff working on the same technology on the same projects for the same users but working for a new employer. The only advantage would appear to be the development approach and the management offered by the outsourcing agency. Why cannot the Information Systems department improve its development style and erode the competitive advantage of external competitors? What is the cost of **not** improving?

In many industries there are examples of the use of information delivering competitive advantage. On the first fast-track project one of us did, the client refused to let us reference their success. They wanted to keep the system secret from their competitors. In the UK in the late 1980s there grew up a very competitive market for telephone quotations for motor insurance. One successful entrant in that market went one better than existing competitors who required you to return a proposal form. They would insure you instantly over the telephone if you gave them a credit card number, because they could create a proposal directly from their information systems, based on the information you gave them. Their whole business was built on better information systems than their competitors.

In the past, genuine success stories were relatively rare. Now probably **all** industry segments offer opportunities to get ahead by effective use of information systems. Certainly all segments offer opportunities to fall behind through ineffective use of information systems.

Establish the Viability of the Change Vehicle

Indicators are:

- pilot project
- cost-benefit analysis
- user success stories.

One of the difficulties in adopting new technology and new ways of working is proving it will be cost effective. The trouble is we cannot prove the concept without making the investment, and we are unwilling to make the investment until the concept is proven. How can we break this vicious circle? Cost-benefit analysis can establish a theoretical business case.

Finding other organizations that have successfully made the move can establish that it is possible and provide an opportunity to learn lessons.

Another, more persuasive way of making the case may be to pilot the approach before committing fully to it. Make a small investment in a suitable project with the right developers and users. If it works well, then the case is made, and the change has started. If the result is less conclusive, then the investment is justified by the implemented pilot project and we have learned some valuable lessons. But with the right people and a suitable project, the pilot project should produce sufficiently encouraging results to maintain and build the momentum of change.

Establish the Skills Base

Indicators are:

- pilot follow-ons
- skills transfer
- recruitment
- training.

Once the need for change is established and the means for change is proven, we need to build momentum. The people who succeeded on the pilot project are now the seed corn for successful implementation.

These developers will be a key resource in the department. Resist the temptation to use them only as a high-profile specialist team. Let them transfer their skills as experts, one on each of the next generation of projects. These pioneers had better have been among the best and most highly respected staff, because now they are the technical leaders, formally or informally, on multiple projects in the department. But skills transfer alone will not be enough. Back them up with formal training and when recruiting try to find people to broaden the growing skills base, or at least people who want to be part of that process. And remember, if you are recruiting fast-track skills so are others. Act to retain your growing skills base. Recognition, and it need not solely be money, cements the loyalty of your key resources and encourages other developers to acquire the same valued skills.

The sponsor of and stakeholders in the pilot project are your ambassadors in the user community. A remote senior management insisting that requirements workshops must be attended will do more harm than good. An enthusiastic operational department demonstrating and talking about the value of their new system will quickly generate interest and a desire to follow suit.

Establish Best Practice

Indicators are:

- template projects
- estimating guidelines
- centres of excellence
- post-implementation reviews
- change as the norm.

Soon there will be a body of success stories, maybe small, maybe not one hundred percent at first. The next step is to make success routine: to identify which variations work best, who are the emerging gurus, how much improvement can we realistically expect, and to make this information available. This can take the form of template project plans that can be reused, for example, based on the tasks and deliverables chapters of this book. It will include standards and guidelines for particular techniques. It will include metrics for estimating, based on experience from previous projects, and a means for managing key resources so they are available for critical tasks across a number of projects.

When this new model for systems development is working, there will be no time for sitting back to admire our handiwork. The change was necessary to adapt to new technology and new expectations of Information Systems effectiveness. These trends will not halt. We must be continually looking to identify the next change and adapting accordingly. Chapter 1 discussed the emergence of fast-track as an evolution from earlier methodologies to take advantage of new technologies, but those technologies are themselves evolving. So effective systems development approaches must also change. It is a continuous process, both in the theory and in the practice in each and every Information Systems department that wants to succeed.

Start Today

Indicators are:

- opportunities in the application backlog
- skills and aptitude in the workforce
- enthusiasm from user sponsors.

The critical success factors for change are not just technology, maybe not even technology. They lie in the organization itself, in the Information Systems department and the user departments that represent its customers. If these people do not feel the need for change and do not share a vision of how to achieve change then no amount of technology and investment will solve the problem. Seek out those people in user departments and in the Information Systems department who can pilot the approach, people who want to succeed and have the potential to succeed. These people will champion the cause of change, because they see the benefits. No change is easy, but it is impossible without the will to change. Start small and demonstrate benefits. Those benefits will generate enthusiasm. That enthusiasm will advertise the benefits and the ball will begin to roll.

In Conclusion

This book has been mostly about technology and techniques, but experience teaches us that the human factor is just as important. Unfortunately, it is not possible to reduce the human factor to words and pictures. What is possible and what hopefully this book has achieved is to provide some help with the technology and techniques and maybe to spark a little of that essential enthusiasm.

A

TIMESAVING HINTS & TIPS

This appendix provides a variety of useful ways to speed up the process, whether it be modelling requirements, design or just 'getting things done' more quickly. The topics covered are:

- Basic techniques
- Information modelling
- Function modelling

Basic Techniques

In the section "Scoping the Project" on page 19 we discussed factors that affect the risk level of a project; these include familiarity with the tools and techniques of fast-track. So the first tip is easy. If the team do not already have skills in information modelling, functional modelling, the use of the tools and other techniques mentioned in Chapter 3, the risks are high. To overload a project with this additional learning curve is too dangerous.

But, beyond the basic techniques there are many other 'soft' skills that help you to be more effective in using those techniques.

Observation and Questioning

A systems analyst who was wandering around a grain store unit noticed that the staff scribbled extra notes on the forms that they were using. The designers of those forms could be forgiven for assuming that when a ton of grain was transferred from one silo to another, what was in the second silo after transfer and what was left behind could be determined by simple arithmetic. Not so – the problem was grain that was blown away during transfer and the changing weight of the grain owing to loss or gain of moisture. These figures were not reflected in the paper system in use which meant that the grain store staff had additional work to do and lower confidence in the system.

Studying the existing forms would not have led to the right solution, and even involving grain store staff in workshops might have missed the right line of questions. Seeing the business in operation and thinking hard about what you see is a great way to identify those extra **'why?'**, **'when?'** and **'how?'** questions that mean you get right to the heart of the requirement.

Guesswork

Guesswork is often frowned upon by 'analysts' who believe that if you have not been told about something or been given details about it, then it cannot be true. That is all very well, but what is usually called systems analysis is in fact two processes, firstly analysis of **what is** and secondly synthesis of **what is required**. Guessing within a logical framework can speed up the process enormously, but always check with the users. Common sense, lay knowledge and the use of parallels from other similar areas (or sometimes even radically different areas) can often trigger off excellent questions that really seek out the essence of what is needed.

Review

Prototyping is one of the most important aspects of fast-track, but a prototype adds no value until it has been reviewed. Review prototypes early and frequently, ideally with users, but before you even get to the users try to explain your design decisions to a colleague or anyone. If you cannot justify the prototype to the cat, the review session with the chief financial officer tomorrow is going to be tricky.

Dry-run Models

Always try to base reviews on real-life examples, and not just simple ones. Include regular exceptions, unusual situations, extreme limits, coexistence and transitional issues, and so on. But it is amazing how much can be learned by dry-running these tests through models, preferably with a user in attendance to help you and to keep things realistic and balanced.

Glossary

Keep a glossary of terms evolving during these activities. The simple act of defining them can resolve issues quickly, identify new problems and take you part of the way forward to providing documentation for your system (for example, with in-context help).

Database

Assume that when you implement you can use a single shared database. This will simplify dataflows, stored files and, as a consequence, the management functions that need to be carried out to maintain them.

Information Modelling

Although information modelling involves well-defined and formal techniques, in practice it is an interactive and evolutionary process. Entity models are usually best produced with a colleague, with a user or in a group.

The process is simple:

- identify a handful of entities at a time
- add relationships and names
- dry-run a few realistic examples
- modify the model based on the issues raised
- expand the scope, a few entities at a time
- add at least two attributes to each entity, starting from reference entities
- put in new type/category/classification/group entities
- add recursive hierarchies
- allow for changes over time
- ensure any object can only be represented by one box
- at every opportunity get the users and your colleagues to help you correct, refine, simplify and add rules to the model
- check that all functions required have the information they need
- check against documents and systems currently in use
- define domains
- consider the life-cycle of important entities
- define unique identifiers for all entities
- minimize the use of arcs and sub-types
- define obvious constraints
- check again with the users.

The same patterns turn up again and again in radically different business areas. You can achieve a great deal in an hour or two by applying raw modelling experience to any model, developing and testing it from various perspectives, as above.

Functional Modelling

In functional modelling, as in information modelling, practical experience suggests that a mixed group of users and experienced systems modellers can rapidly construct, test and hone functional models.

Take a major business process or functional area and then:

- identify the key event in the business and the required outcome
- write down a list of functions that cover this life-cycle

- examine the list and look for exceptions

- check for other related events and other possible outcomes

- draw a flat dataflow model of the area

- guess the input and output flows of data and any possible intermediate datastores

- cross-check against the entity model and update both models to correspond to each other

- re-check the whole with the other users and correct the terms

- add functions to maintain (i.e., create, retrieve, update and delete) reference information.

Summary

A common mistake that modellers make is to try to create the perfect model. This leads to spending an excessive amount of time on small areas of the scope. It is better to take a broader perspective and to use the guesswork/dry-run/review cycle to iteratively refine the models. Use the information model to test the function model and use the function model to test the information model. Above all, involve users and colleagues to evolve the solution rather than try to create perfection in isolation.

Appendix

B

Using Other Books in the CASE Method Series

At the time of writing, there are three other books in the series which are complementary to this one. This appendix gives an indication of some of the most useful ways of using them in association with a fast-track project.

CASE Method Tasks and Deliverables

This book covers a comprehensive approach to completing the full life-cycle of any project and is especially targeted at systems that are large, complex, interrelated or need special control. It is worth reading the first two introductory chapters in full and skip-reading the first three or four pages of Chapters 3 to 9. This will ensure that you have a good grasp of the basic objectives and outcomes of the more traditional stages in the life-cycle – Strategy, Analysis, Design, and so on. If you have more time, the most important areas to concentrate on are strategy, where what needs to be done is established, and transition, which must be performed correctly to achieve system acceptance.

Chapter 10 on project management is useful particularly for the ideas on risk management, key resource management, and so on, but do be careful not to fall into the trap of putting on too many controls. Fast-track is all about trusting competent people to get it right, with light control and with quality, in all senses of the word, being assured by rapid regular communication among the right group of empowered people.

Quality is covered extensively in the Tasks and Deliverables book, with a chapter on quality assurance, an appendix of checklists, and quality notes against each task. If you skip-read through these you will know what is covered and when it will be useful to go to the book for guidance.

When you do encounter a problem or some complex area, go to the relevant section in the Tasks and Deliverables and more often than not you will find useful guidance.

CASE Method Entity Relationship Modelling

This book is an important companion to a fast-track approach, as the richness and accuracy of the model when used with the CASE tool can help you make enormous productivity and quality gains.

At least one person on a fast-track team should be an expert in entity relationship modelling and have learned on a small, real and reasonably complex example how a model can, on the one hand, reflect a user need and, on the other hand, be used to generate both a database design and much of the client- or server-side code.

At least one other member of the project should be reasonably competent at entity modelling. This person would find the following chapters and appendices of most use: Chapters 1 to 7 and 10, and Appendices A on "Data Normalization", B on "Valid Relationships" and F on "Relational Database Design". Other team players who just need a quick overall understanding should read Chapters 1, 2 and 4.

CASE Method Function and Process Modelling

The fast-track approach concentrates on using just two of the many modelling techniques covered in this book, so you will find it particularly useful to read Chapters 1 to 5, which act as an introduction to the basic concepts and cover function decomposition and function hierarchies in depth. Chapter 11 on dataflow diagramming is also essential reading, but remember to concentrate on a non-rigorous dataflow for the overall scope, which will aid communication with your users, and on the lowest level or leaf dataflows, which will be used much more rigorously to drive the CASE generators.

If you find that these two techniques are insufficient on your project, Chapter 15 on "When to Use What" is very useful. Appendices A on "Quality and Completeness Checks", B on "Valid Constructs" and E on "Commonly Occurring and Forgotten Functions" will all help you speed up the process.

At least two members of the team need to be proficient in function decomposition, dataflow diagramming and how these models are used by the CASE tools to generate code. One person should also have at least an overview of the other techniques for modelling functions, so that if a case arises where it would be more productive to apply one of these the team member will recognize the need and know where to go for help.

And finally, a word of guidance. When carrying out a fast-track project, experience shows that it is effective and pragmatic to blur the distinction that the Function and Process Modelling book makes between a function – what the business does, irrespective of how it does it – and a mechanism – which is a particular way of carrying out a business function. For example, 'Ascertain unique identifier for a person's Frequent Traveller Programme' is a business function. A fast-track definition might be 'Swipe frequent flyer card to get passenger's frequent flyer number'.

BIBLIOGRAPHY

Barker, R. *et al.* (1990). *CASE*Method Tasks and Deliverables*. Wokingham, England, Addison-Wesley.

Barker, R. (1990). *CASE*Method Entity Relationship Modelling*. Wokingham, England, Addison-Wesley.

Barker, R. and Longman, C. (1993). *CASE*Method Function and Process Modelling*. Wokingham, England, Addison-Wesley.

Belasco, J. (1990). *Teaching the Elephant to Dance*. England, Random House.

Billings, C. and Billings, M. (1993). *Rapid Development with Oracle CASE, A Workshop Approach*. Reading, Massachusetts, Addison-Wesley.

Boehm, B. (1988). A Spiral Model of Software Development and Enhancement. *COMPUTER*, **21**(5), 61–72.

Budde, R. *et al.* (1991). *Prototyping, An Approach to Evolutionary System Development*. Berlin, Springer-Verlag.

Gane, C. (1987). *Rapid Systems Development*. USA, RSDI.

Hickman, C. (1990). *Mind of a Manager, Soul of a Leader*. New York, John Wiley & Sons.

Martin, J. (1991). *Rapid Application Development*. USA, Macmillan.

Oracle Corporation (1994a). *Oracle CASE Dictionary Reference Manual*.

Oracle Corporation (1994b). *Oracle Generator for Forms Reference Manual*.

Oracle Corporation (1994c). *Oracle Generator for Reports Reference Manual*.

Peters, T. (1987). *Thriving on Chaos*. USA, Alfred A Knopf.

Reiss, G. (1992). *Project Management Demystified*. London, C & F N Spon.

Symons, C.R. (1991). *Software Sizing and Estimating, Mk II FPA*. London, John Wiley & Sons.

Yourdon, E. and Constantine, L. (1975). *Structured Design*. USA, Yourdon Press.

GLOSSARY OF TERMS

Actuals Information gathered during a project concerning the actual amount of time or other effort expended on a task.

Application A screen program, report, utility program or other self-contained program unit that may be used to assist the user in a task she or he is performing, possibly by accessing and/or manipulating stored data.

Application System A name given to a collection of business functions, entities, programs and tables, which may be further described by system documentation of various forms. It will typically be used to describe a coherent unit of work; for example, a project, sub-system or data subject area.

Arc A means of identifying two or more mutually exclusive relationships.

Association A significant relationship between elements of the same or different type within a CASE environment. See also **Element**.

Atomic Function A business function that is not further decomposed into consistent business functions once analysis of the function is complete. Also known as a Leaf Function.

Attribute Any detail that serves to qualify, identify, classify, quantify or express the state of an entity **or** any description of 'a thing of significance'. Note that each entity occurrence may only have one value of any attribute at one time.

Business An enterprise, commercial house or firm in either the private or public sector, concerned with providing products and/or services to satisfy customer requirements; for example, a car manufacturer, a refuse collection company, a legal advice provider, an organization providing health care.

Business Analyst A person whose job is to investigate, understand and document how an organization works. The normal use of this analysis is in the construction of information systems.

Business Function What a business or enterprise does or needs to do, irrespective of how it does it. See also **Elementary Business Function.**

Business Function Model A representation of all the business functions within a defined scope. A wide range of techniques is available for modelling business functions. In fast-track projects, hierarchies which break down business functions recursively are the primary technique used. See

Function Decomposition and **Function Hierarchy.**

Business Location   A uniquely identifiable geographic location, site or place from which one or more business units may be wholly or partly operating.

Business Model   A collection of models representing a definition of a business. Components include models of objectives, functions and information. See **Entity Relationship Diagram** and **Business Function Model.**

Business Objective   A statement of business intent that may be measured quantitatively. A quantifiable goal or target. Aims and objectives are similar concepts but the achievement of an objective is measurable in some specific manner; for example, to increase profitability by 1% during the next financial year.

Business Priority   A statement of important business need or requirement within an ordered list.

Business Process Re-engineering   The activity by which an enterprise defines its goals and the processes by which it attempts to achieve them and redesigns and re-implements those processes. This can result in radically improved human and computer systems, which remove redundant activities, streamline and optimize resource utilization.

Business Rule   A constraint under which an organization operates. It may be a physical constraint, a legal constraint, a policy or other constraint. Also known as a constraint or a business constraint.

For example; '*We cannot take a booking for more than 300 rooms concurrently*' (physical constraint imposed by the size of the hotel). '*We must offer free delivery for local orders*' (a policy responding to competitive pressures).

Business System Life-Cycle   A definition of the process of developing and maintaining computer systems such that business needs drive the development rather than technology. (Also called the Development Life-Cycle.)

Business Unit   Part of an organization which is treated for any purpose as a separate unit within the parent organization; for example, a department.

CASE   Computer-Aided Systems Engineering is the combination of graphical, repository, generator, project management and other software tools to assist computer development staff engineer and maintain high-quality systems for their end users, within the framework of a methodical approach. Sometimes referred to as Computer-Aided Software Engineering.

Change Request   A change to the required behaviour of a system, usually from a user as a result of reviewing current behaviour. Change requests need careful management, because what looks like a simple change to make can have a far-reaching impact elsewhere. See also **Impact Analysis** and **Flip-flop.**

Client/Server   The use of information systems that link many personal computers and/or workstations (clients) to fewer large processors (servers). The clients generally manage the user interface, possibly with some local data. This is known as the client-side processing. Servers usually manage multiple access databases, including data integrity and other invariants, the server-side processing.

Code Generator   See **Generator**.

Column   A means of implementing an item of data in a table.

Configuration Management   The process of managing hardware, software, data and any other documentation needed during the development, testing and implementation of information systems.

Constraint   See **Business Rule.**

Context Diagram   A picture, usually in the syntax of a dataflow diagram, indicating the major functional components and major internal and external interdependencies of a system.

Critical Success Factor   Any business event, dependency, deliverable or other factor which, if not attained, would seriously impair the likelihood of achieving a business objective.

Coupling and Cohesion   Coupling indicates the degree to which project partitions share data or control information. Loose coupling is desirable and broadly means that the two partitions only share database data, but are otherwise independent. Cohesion is a measure of the extent to which modules within a partition are related to one another. High cohesion is desirable and implies that the partition is supporting a single complete process from start to finish.

Custom code   Coding added to a generated module or program to implement functionality that the generator has not provided.

Database   An arbitrary collection of tables or files under the control of a database management system.

Data Definition   The specification of an element of data to be maintained. The specification will include data type, size and rules about the processing: for example, derivation and validation. See also **Business Rule** and **Invariant**.

Data Definition Language (DDL)   A language for defining and manipulating the structure and form of a database, rather than its contents. For example, 'Create Index', 'Alter Table' are fragments of SQL DDL.

Dataflow   A named collection of entities, attributes, relationships and as yet unformalized information (data items) passing from one place to another. A dataflow connects a function and either another function or a datastore or an external entity. See **Business Function**, **Datastore** and **External Entity**.

Dataflow Diagram   A diagram representing the use of data by business functions or processes. See **Dataflow**, **Datastore** and **External Entity**.

Datastore   A named collection of entities, attributes, relationships and as yet unformalized information (data items), as used by specified business functions, which needs to be retained over a period of time. Storage may be temporary or permanent. During the early stage of analysis a datastore may contain data items which are subsequently converted to attributes.

DBMS   Database management system, normally encompassing computerized management facilities that are used to structure and manipulate data, and to ensure privacy, recovery and integrity in a multi-user environment. Databases operate by different data modelling paradigms, such as relational, and manipulate numbers, text, dates, sound, images, drawings, documents, video, and so on.

Deliverable   Something that is produced by a task of a project or produced by an external agency for use in the project. See also **Prerequisite**.

Denormalization   Data modelling techniques such as Entity Relationship modelling lead to database designs which are normalized. That is to say the information in them is recorded once, and once only, and cross-related to all other relevant data. This provides a very flexible design, which may not be optimal for particular processes. Denormalization is the design activity which restructures the database, introducing derived data, replicated data and repeating data to tune the system to meet some specific performance goal or goals.

Design Prototype   The first working version of a fast-track system. It is normally generated directly from the models built during the Requirements Stage.

Distributed Database A database that is physically located on more than one computer processor, connected via some form of communications network. An essential feature of a distributed database is that the user and/or program work as if they had access to the whole database locally. All processing to give this impression is carried out by the database management system.

Distributed Processing The ability to have more than one computer working together in a network, where each processor can be used to perform different parts of the required processing for a user.

Domain A set of validation rules, format constraints and other properties that apply to a group of attributes and/or database columns.

For example:

- a list of values
- a range
- a qualified list or range
- any combination of these.

See also **Business Rule**.

Element An element, in CASE, is a thing of significance about which system developers need to record information in order to define a system requirement and implementation. Elements are further described by properties and associations to other elements. For example, you may need to record information about three tables (each of which is an occurrence of an element) and two program modules (two occurrences of a different element). The association between them would be which program uses which table and how. A company may often need to extend a repository by adding new elements, properties and associations.

Element Type Any element held in the repository is classified as being of a particular type.

Examples of element type are entity, attribute, program module, process, table, diagram, text, softbox. Occurrences or instances of these are called elements.

Elementary Business Function A business function which, if started, must be completed successfully or, if for some reason it cannot be completed successfully, any changes it makes up to the point of failure must be undone, as though they had never happened. See **Function Hierarchy.**

End User The person for whom a system is being developed; for example, an airline reservations clerk is an end user of an airline reservations system. See **Stakeholder** and **Sponsor**.

Entity A thing of significance, whether real or imagined, about which information needs to be known or held. See **Attribute**.

Entity Integrity Rules The rules that specify valid values or combination of values for the attributes of an entity. These may include unique identifiers, domains and multi-attribute validation rules and represent single entity business rules. At the system level, these correspond to keys, table constraints and column constraints. See also **Referential Integrity Constraint** and **Business Rule**.

Entity Relationship Diagram A part of the business model that defines the information to be managed and processed. Produced during requirements definition, the diagram pictorially represents entities, the vital business relationships between them and the attributes used to describe them. See **Entity**, **Attribute** and **Relationship**.

The process of creating this diagram is called entity modelling. The terms entity model, entity relationship model and entity/relationship model are all synonyms for Entity Relationship Diagram.

Event A thing that happens or takes place, or an outcome or result: the arrival of a significant point in time, a change in status of something, or the occurrence of something external that causes the business to react. There are four types of event, external, change, time and system, all of which may act as triggers to one or more business functions.

External Change   A change to a part of a system under development which will have an impact on the development of other parts of the system or other systems. In fast-track external changes are those that affect other partitions. See also **Impact Analysis**, **Change Request** and **Project Partition.**

External Entity   A thing of significance, outside the scope of the application system, that acts as a source or recipient of dataflows. An external entity might be a person, a business unit, another application system, or any other thing that might provide or receive information from a function within the application system.

Facilitator   The person in a feedback session or workshop who has the job of ensuring that all aspects of the topic under discussion are properly explored and that the understanding and requirements of the users are reflected in the notes and models of the scribe. See also **Workshop.**

Feedback   Response, including corrections, additions and approval, elicited from users, stakeholders, sponsors and others, to a system specification, design, plan or implementation.

Feedback Session   A meeting organized to present work in progress in order to gain feedback. See **Feedback**.

Flip-flop   The undesirable situation where a stakeholder suggests an alternative implementation of a requirement, but when presented with the alternative, prefers the original, and vice versa.

Foreign Key   One or more columns in a relational database table that implement a many-to-one or a one-to-one relationship that the table in question has with another table or itself. This concept allows the database to join the two tables together and access the combined data in a single instruction (normally a statement of SQL).

Formal Build   Construction of an information system by the well-established steps of specify/ code/test/correct. See also **Iterative Build**.

Fourth-Generation Programming Language (4GL)   A language that manipulates high-level objects, such as screen items and database tables, by declaring what is to be done to them rather than procedurally describing how it is to be done, as in 3GLs. See also **3GL**.

Function Decomposition   A technique for modelling business functions by decomposing a single business function into a number of lower level business functions, and then progressively decomposing these until the appropriate level of detail is reached. Function decomposition gives rise to functions arranged in groups/hierarchies known as a business function hierarchy. See also **Elementary Business Function**, **Function Hierarchy** and **Atomic Function**.

Function Hierarchy   A simple grouping of functions in a strict hierarchy, representing all the functions in an area of a business. This forms part of the business model produced during requirements definition. See also **Business Function** and **Function Decomposition**.

Function Point Analysis (FPA)   A method of measuring the size of information systems (their function point counts) in terms of data usages and processing complexities, adjusted for environmental factors. Consistent function point counts allow an organization to establish productivity measures to assist in estimating.

Generator   A mechanism for transforming the specification of a module into executable program code. Also known as a code generator.

Generator Template   A skeleton or outline program from which a generator can reuse common elements.

For example, boilerplate information, window sizes, 'OK' and 'Quit' buttons, and others.

Group Interview   Any session where stakeholders or sponsors collectively discuss the requirements, design or implementation of an information system. See Feedback and **Workshop**.

Impact Analysis   The process of understanding what the effects would be elsewhere in a system of making a particular change.

For example, what modules would need revising if we want to record a Guest Name of up to 60 characters instead of the current limit of 40.

Index   An access mechanism to documents or data. A means of accessing one or more rows in a database table.

Industry Template   An outline definition of systems to support a specific industry or business process, for example a customer service template. An industry template will consist of information and activity models, a statement about the business process and may include demonstrations, prototypes and so on.

Information System   A system for managing and processing information, usually computer based.

Information Systems (IS) Department   That part of an organization responsible for identifying and implementing the appropriate information systems to support the needs of the organization.

Instance See **Type and Instance.**

Interim Deliverable   A deliverable which is not required at the completion of a task, but which is useful as a milestone within the task, for progress monitoring or for review. See also **Deliverable.**

Invariant   A rule about how information is validated or processed which is always true, no matter what the context. See also **Business Rule.**

Iterative Build   Incremental construction of an information system by means of a cycle of code/test/review, starting from a prioritized outline definition and guided by user feedback.

Iterative Development   The application of a cyclic, evolutionary approach to the development of requirements definition, design or construction using prototyping and iterative build techniques.

Key   A way of accessing something. Any set of columns that is frequently used for retrieval of rows from a table. See also **Unique Identifier** and **Primary Key**.

Key Resource   A person with a wide range of skills and/or experiences who can be effective in many types of task.

Key Result   The outcome a business is trying to achieve upon receipt of an event.

Legacy System   An existing information system which it is now difficult to support and maintain because of changes in technology or business processes.

Look and Feel   The appearance and behaviour of a system facility as perceived by the user. This will include the data, the layout and the user interaction, through menus, buttons, text editing and other devices.

Look and Feel Guidelines   Standards for how the look and feel of facilities should be implemented in order to ensure consistency. See also **Look and Feel** and **Style Guide.**

Matrix Diagram   A spreadsheet style diagram where the axes represent two associated types of element of interest to information systems developers.

For example, a matrix of modules against modules indicating, in the cells, which module calls and is called by which others.

Mechanism A particular technique or technology for implementing a function. Examples might be a telephone, a computer, an electronic mail service.

Module A procedure that implements one or more business functions, or parts of business functions, within a computer system. A module is often implemented by a computer program.

MoSCoW **M**ust have, **S**hould have, **C**ould have, **W**on't have, a way of classifying and prioritizing facilities for inclusion in an information system. Used in timeboxed development where the scope may need to be redefined according to the rate of progress.

Module Network A module may be broken down into sub-modules. A module may be used as a sub-module of several others (e.g. a common subroutine). By this means a network of modules may be created.

Network An interconnected network of computers as referred to in distributed processing. May also be used to mean module network.

Node A computer network has a series of nodes. Each node would normally represent a single computer or group of computers or a mechanism for handling communication traffic **or**

The word node is occasionally used to represent a particular instance of a function on a Function Hierarchy Diagram.

Normalization A step-by-step process that produces either entity or table definitions that have:

- no multi-valued attributes or columns
- the same kind of values assigned to all occurrences of any given attribute or column

- a unique name
- uniquely identifiable rows.

Null Some database management systems allow a column, field or data item to hold a value that means 'there is no current value'; this is known as a null value.

Object Orientation (OO) The perspective that systems should be constructed from objects, which themselves may be aggregations of smaller objects. An object represents any concept or thing in the real world, for example a button on a screen or a customer account. An object definition includes all the information known about the real-world thing (in this way it is similar to an entity) and all the behaviours of that real-world thing.

For example, a customer account would know which customer it was for, whether it was a cash or credit account and also how to perform a credit check, create a new account, close the account and so on. See also **Type and Instance**.

Object Technology (OT) The technology, programming languages, development tools, databases and so on, introduced to support object-oriented systems development.

Outsourcing The practice of appointing an external organization to provide the services of the IS department or any other internal service department.

Prerequisite Something needed by a task of a project that is produced by a previous task or an external agency. See also **Deliverable**.

Prescriptive Methodology A methodology or method which instructs the systems developer what to do at each step, attempting to eliminate the possibility of human error. Prescriptive methodologies are successful in organizations where experience and skill levels are relatively low.

Priority See **Business Priority**.

Primary Key   A set of one or more columns in a database table whose values, in combination, are required to be unique within the table. If there is more than one such combination of columns that will guarantee uniqueness then one is arbitrarily declared the primary key. The others are known as Unique Keys. The primary key is usually selected as the one most frequently used. See also **Key**.

Project Baseline   A project plan which is retained as a reference point for comparison with what actually happens later.

Project Coordinator   A person authorized to resolve any conflict that may arise during the project. This may be the project sponsor, but he or she may not have sufficient in-depth knowledge of the operations to perform this task unaided.

Project Earned Value   A measure of the value of completed tasks in a project. There are various ways of measuring the value of a task. These include percentage on commencement, percentage on completion, amount at milestone.

Project Milestone   A significant point in a project whose arrival can be recognized, for example, by the completion of a task or the availability of a deliverable. Milestones are defined as measures of progress.

Project Objectives   The set of criteria by which a project's success will be measured.

Project Partition   Part of a project. Usually representing a coherent set of facilities to be developed by a single developer.

Project Schedule   A specification of work to be done together with allocation of resources and times to the tasks.

Project Template   An outline project plan which can be reused as the basis of a specific plan. A project template normally identifies the tasks, major deliverables, the dependencies between the tasks and guidelines for estimating the tasks.

Prototyping   The construction of a partial system to demonstrate some aspect or aspects of the intended system behaviour in order to gain user acceptance or to establish technical feasibility.

Quick Build See **Iterative Development**.

Rapid Application Development (RAD)   An approach to information systems development which relies heavily on user interaction: for example in workshops to establish needs and by iterative development to demonstrate development direction. CASE Method Fast-track is a RAD approach.

RDBMS   Relational database management system.

Referential Integrity Constraint   The rules which specify the correspondence of a foreign key to the primary key of its related table.

For example, what should happen to the foreign key when the referenced primary key row is deleted. See also **Business Rule**.

Regression Testing   A technique for retesting a system after a change has been made to ensure that no side effects have been introduced. Regression testing makes use of test plans whose results are known for the pre-change system. These plans should produce the same results afterwards.

Relationship   What one thing has to do with another **or** any significant way in which two things of the same or different type may be associated.

Repository   A mechanism for storing any information to do with the definition of a system at any point in its life-cycle. Repository services would typically be provided for extensibility, recovery, integrity, naming standards, and a wide variety of other management functions.

Requirements Prototype   A way of evolving a definition of the scope for a proposed information system by producing and refining a prototype. The prototype itself will probably be discarded. Its purpose is to illustrate what is possible and to clarify the scope and priorities of the users' requirements.

Requirements Workshop   A workshop, usually attended by project sponsor, stakeholders and developers, with the objective of providing a sufficiently detailed definition for a developer to commence build. The definition will be further defined and refined during development and particularly by user reviews. See also **Workshop** and **User Review.**

Resource Database   A record of the resources available, usually primarily the human resources, often including information about the skills and experiences of the resources to improve the match of skills to task.

Resource Management   The task of making the best use of available resources, usually human, such that the optimal balance of short-term objectives and longer-term skills and career development goals are met. What is optimal across the whole resource pool may not be optimal for an individual project or person.

Reverse Engineering   The automatic creation of system specifications from existing code and data definitions. Never complete, because we cannot know why a particular implementation was chosen just from looking at the code, but often useful for impact analysis and the design of a replacement system. See also **Impact Analysis**.

Risk Adaptive Management   The practice of recognizing, assessing and planning for risks, as opposed to attempting to avoid or eliminate risk entirely.

Row   An entry in a database table that typically corresponds to an instance of some real thing, consisting of a set of values for all mandatory columns and relevant optional columns. A row is often an implementation of an instance of an entity. See also **Table** and **Column**.

Schedule   See **Project Schedule**.

Schema   An information model that can be implemented in a database. The schema may be a logical schema, which will define, for example, tables, columns and constraints, but which may not include any optimization. Or it may be a physical schema that includes optimization, for example, table clustering.

Scope Creep   The common phenomenon where additional requirements are added after a project has started without reconsidering the resourcing or timescale of the project. Scope creep arises from the misapprehension that such additions will not affect the project schedule because each individual addition is small.

Scoping Workshop   A workshop, usually attended by the project sponsor and developers, with the objective of defining the boundaries of the scope for an intended project prioritizing requirements within the scope. See also **Workshop**.

Scribe   The role in a workshop with responsibility for ensuring that all relevant comments are noted. These comments may well be translated into formal models and possibly entered directly into CASE tools.

Server Side   See **Client/Server.**

Skills Database   See **Resource Database.**

Spaghetti Code   Program logic that is badly structured. Often the result of many small modifications so that the original design has become lost in the amendments and fixes. So called because a diagram of the logic paths through such a piece of code would resemble a plate of spaghetti.

Sponsor   That user who is the final arbiter on all matters concerning the project. Commonly the person who holds the budget for the project, or the appointee of the budget holder.

SQL   Structured Query Language.   The ANSI (American National Standards Institute) internationally accepted standard for relational database systems, covering not only query but also data definition, manipulation, security and some aspects of referential and entity integrity.

Stakeholder   A user who has been given responsibility to approve or request modification of a part of a system under development. Commonly there is one stakeholder per partition. A stakeholder is usually a respected and experienced member of the end-user population for whom that partition is being developed.

Stub Module   A module in a partially developed system which performs no function other than perhaps to display a message that it has been invoked. A stub module is used to represent a module yet to be developed. Stub modules are useful in user reviews to indicate the point at which a particular facility would be invoked.

Style Guide   A collection of examples and rules which exist to assist developers in building systems which have consistency: in appearance to the end user, in behaviour, in structure and in documentation. Style guides may be automated in CASE and other program development tools. See also **Look and Feel Guidelines** and **User Preferences**.

System   A named, defined and interacting collection of real-world facts, procedures and processes, along with the organized deployment of people, machines, various mechanisms and other resources that carry out those procedures and processes. See also **Application System**.

System Architecture   A graphical or pictorial representation of the structure of a system. Usually confined to essentials only, and in fast-track systems, normally just a hierarchical diagram of the system, sub-systems and modules arranged as they would be viewed by the user.

System Facility   A part of an information system that supports an identifiable set of business functions. A facility may be a single module or it may be a whole sub-system.

Table   A view of data, used in a relational database management system, defined by one or more columns of data and a primary key. A table would be populated by rows of data. It is often an implementation of an entity.

Table Constraint   A set of rules constraining values in a combination of one or more columns of a database table. If the constraint is that the combined values must be unique, then the constraint is known as a Unique Key or Primary Key. Table constraints are a means of implementing some business rules.

Template   See **Project Template, Industry Template** and **Generator Template.**

Test Harness   A combination of software and possibly hardware which provides a stable environment in which newly developed software can be tested without elaborate preparation. A test harness might provide test data, data structures, test scripts, automatic test execution, test results recording and test results analysis.

Third-Generation Programming Language (3GL)   A language that uses procedural definitions for the tasks to be carried out, and typically uses record-by-record processing of data.

Procedural 3GL language structures include 'if...then...else', 'do...while' and others.

Timebox   A project, or sub-project, which has dedicated assigned resources and a fixed end date. The contingency for under-estimation of the work is provided by a prioritized list of features that can be left out if necessary. The contingency for over-estimation is provided by a prioritized list of features that should be added in if time allows.

Transformer   A utility that takes as input one section of a CASE system model and creates another part of the model from it.

For example, a utility that creates a relational database design from an entity relationship model.

Trigger   In CASE Method the word trigger is used in the sense that an event will trigger one or more functions or that a function may be triggered by the completion of another function (an implied event). See **Event**.

In database terms, a trigger is a piece of code executed by a database management system when a defined action occurs; for example, when a row is inserted into a table. Database triggers provide a means of implementing business rules. For example, when we record a guest room allocation we also create an entry in the room cleaning roster for the appropriate floor.

Type and Instance   The same word is often used to represent a type (or class) of thing and an instance (or occurrence) of a thing.

For example, the word Car may be used in the sense of a model or type of car; an instance of this would be uniquely identified by the name 'Silver Cloud Rolls-Royce'. The word Car may also be used in the sense of defining a vehicle; an instance of this would be a Silver Cloud Rolls-Royce uniquely identified by the registration number 'WRB 1'. In a database one might find two tables: one called MODEL, which has, say, a hundred rows each corresponding to the hundred types of models of cars that we know of; the other called CAR, which has, say, twenty thousand rows, each of which corresponds to an actual vehicle.

Unique Identifier   A combination of attributes and/or relationships that serves, in all cases, to uniquely identify an occurrence of an entity, **or**

Any combination of columns that serves, in all cases, to uniquely identify an occurrence of a row in a table.

Primary keys and unique indexes are alternative ways of implementing unique identifiers on a relational database management system.

Unit Testing   Testing a program or module alone, using predefined test data to represent any inputs from previous processes or interfaces.

Usability   That quality of a system that makes it easy to learn, easy to use and encourages the user to regard the system as a positive help in getting the job done.

User Preferences   In many circumstances in computer systems there may be alternative ways a user can influence the behaviour of a utility, user interface or other system process. These may typically be set by adjusting values in a set of user preferences; for example, in a program generator, preferences may be used to implement a style guide by providing settings for style, performance, user interface behaviour, code standards, and so on.

User Review   A meeting at which some of the facilities of a system are demonstrated to, and tested by, the user. The objective of a user review is to elicit feedback on which to base future development and improvement of the facilities being reviewed.

User Sponsor   See **Sponsor**.

Utility   A program or system facility that performs a useful job for the users, but does not require the user to provide any interaction other than perhaps initially requesting the utility. See also **Transformer** and **Generator.**

View   A means of accessing a subset of the database as if it were a table. The view may:

- be restricted to named columns
- be restricted to specific rows

- change column names
- derive new columns
- give access to a combination of related tables and/or views.

Walkthrough   Review of work in progress, usually taking the form of a presentation by the developer to an audience of stakeholders and/or fellow developers who are encouraged to comment and ask questions. The objective is to ensure that the work is proceeding in the right direction.

Work Package   A unit of work allocated to a developer, defining the scope (what functions or modules) and the tasks (for example design, build and test). Commonly synonymous with a Partition in the build stage of a fast-track project. See also **Project Partition**.

Workshop   A meeting attended by users and developers with the objective of creating a specification or other documentation which can guide the developers in their next task. See also **Scoping Workshop, Requirements Workshop** and **User Review**.

INDEX

A

Activity 49, 59
Actuals 103, 191
Attribute 40, 42, 60, 191

B

Best practice 178
Build
    formal 18, 21, 74, 144–55, 195
    iterative 6, 18, 74, 136–43, 196
    timebox 6, 21
    user-driven 18, 127, 137
Business
    analyst 9, 11, 127, 136, 191
    constraint 192
    effectiveness 175
    function 11, 42, 191
    issues vi
    objective 192
    process vi, 173, 183, 192
    rule vii, 40, 57, 139, 192, 193, 194, 196, 198, 200
    unit 42, 45, 46, 60, 85, 109, 116, 192
Business function model see Model

C

CASE viii, x, 2, 8, 14, 192
CASE Method 2, 3, 6, 15, 185
CASE tools 46, 119, 127
Change request 64, 66, 120, 122, 129, 132, 136, 138, 154, 159, 160, 192
Client/server vi, vii, 39, 112, 113, 186, 192
Cohesion 23, 84, 134, 193
Column 40, 42, 192
Competitive advantage 176
Complexity
    programming 13
    project 13
Computer-Aided Systems Engineering (CASE) viii, x, 2, 8, 14, 192
Configuration management 157, 192
Constraint 192
Context diagram 47, 49, 193
Contingency 30

Convergent prototype see Prototype
Cost-benefit analysis 49, 55, 176
Coupling 23, 84, 134, 193
Critical success factors 178, 193
    Build 129
    Planning 76
    Requirements 99
Cultural change 175
Custom code 137, 169, 193

D

Data
    administration 142, 150
    appearance and behaviour defaults 112, 142, 148, 150
    definition 142, 150, 193
    definition language 193
    migration 165
Database 182, 193
    administration 142
    definition 112, 118
    design 112, 141, 144, 148
    management system 193
    procedures 147
    schema 143, 161
Dataflow diagram 8, 107, 193
DDL see Data definition language
Deliverables ix, 2, 6, 25, 28, 31, 49, 61, 63, 164, 193
    Build 127, 133–63
    interim 25
    Planning 74, 79–93
    Requirements 96, 103–25
Denormalization 160, 193
Dependencies
    Build 131
    external 114
    Requirements 101, 122
    Transition 166
Design
    application 43, 114
    database 39, 112, 141, 160
    index 112
    system architecture 116
    usability 44, 119, 201
Designer 9, 11

Distributed database 194
Divergent prototype see Prototype
Documentation
   system 128
   user 128
Domain 40, 194

E

Elementary business function 42, 43, 46, 60, 109,
   194
Entity 40, 42, 60, 194
Entity relationship diagram 107, 194
Estimating 2, 25, 38, 90, 178
Event 46, 58, 60, 153, 183, 194, 201
External change 138, 140–3, 148–51, 156, 166, 195

F

Facilitator 53, 195
Fast-track ix, 3, 12
   hyper 168
   one-shot 170
Feedback 54, 138, 195
Feedback session 47–8, 78, 195
Flip-flop 69, 129, 158, 195
Fourth-generation programming language 62, 83,
   95, 136, 174, 195
Function decomposition 107, 195
Function point analysis 24, 195

G

Generator 195
   code vi, 8, 11
   technology vii, 5, 18, 61, 119, 127, 137
Graphical user interface vi
Guesswork 182
Guest administration example 4, 9, 11, 20, 21, 30,
   50, 56, 58, 61, 82, 94, 97, 98, 114

H

Hyper fast-track 168

I

IE see Information engineering
Impact analysis 138, 196, 199
Implementation
   CASE 173
   Fast-track 173–9
Implementation specialist 23, 127, 132, 134, 144

Incremental development see Iterative
   development
Index 160, 196
Information Engineering 2, 3
Information systems 1, 196
   department 173, 175, 176, 178, 196
   development 3
   management v
   strategy 73, 78
Interim deliverable 196
Interim milestone 29
Interpersonal skills 32
Invariant 39, 96, 98, 112, 141, 196
Iterative build 18
Iterative development 64, 65, 136, 196

K

Key 40, 196, 198
Key resource 90, 177, 178, 196
Key result 46, 58, 196

L

Language 54
Leadership 32
Legacy system 165, 196
Life-cycle ix, 8, 192
   CASE Method 15, 185
   fast-track 15, 73, 173
   iterative development 65
   spiral 3
   waterfall 2
Look and feel 62, 141, 143, 148, 150, 154, 157, 196

M

Maintenance 155, 170, 171, 175
Matrix diagram 8, 56, 196
Mechanism 187, 197
Method 1, 2, 8, 197
Milestone see Project milestone
Model
   business vi, 192
   business function 42, 46, 97, 191
   data 1
   dataflow 43, 49, 186
   dependency 50
   entity relationship 1, 11, 38, 40, 49, 57, 186, 194
   event 58
   function 11, 23, 38, 41–4, 47, 49, 53, 57, 59, 170,

181, 183–4, 186
information 38–41, 60, 181, 182–3
logical schema 39, 40
system architecture 11, 38, 44–7, 116
Modelling in workshops 58–60
MoSCoW 27, 55, 79, 144, 160, 197
Motivation 7

O

Objective see Business objective and Project
    objectives
One-shot fast-track 170
Oracle Book 153
Oracle CASE viii, x, 14, 43, 71, 147, 175
  change history 139
  column definition 105, 113
  data definition language generator 113, 143
  data usages linking 115
  dataflow diagrammer 85
  default application design utility 115
  default database design utility 113
  default menu design utility 117
  detailed data usage 115
  documents 105, 133, 145, 157, 159
  entity relationship diagrammer 79, 107
  function hierarchy diagrammer 79, 107
  function point count reports 91
  generator for forms 81, 113, 119, 123, 137, 157
  generator for reports 81, 119, 123, 137, 157
  generator preferences 105
  generators 39
  help text 153
  impact analysis reports 141, 155
  keys and constraints 113
  matrix diagrammer 79, 85, 89, 103, 107, 109, 123,
    125, 141, 155, 159
  modelling in 38–47
  module definition 139
  module history 133, 159
  module network 117
  quality and completeness reports 103, 109, 133
  reverse engineering facilities 137, 155
  table definition 139
  templates 105
Oracle Data Query 155
Oracle Forms 62, 83, 137, 147, 155
Oracle Reports 83, 137, 155
Outsourcing 175, 176, 197

P

Packaged system 173
Partition see Project partition

People skills 32
Performance tuning 9, 113, 160, 165, 167, 168
Pilot project 16, 175, 176
PL/SQL 147
Plan
  contingency 30
  project ix, 16, 73, 75, 92, 167
  quality 30, 75, 88, 90
  resource 38, 75
  test 128
Post-implementation review 168, 178
Prioritization 27, 54
Productivity 4, 24, 174, 175
Programmer 9, 11
Project
  baseline 92, 198
  characteristics 20
  complexity 169
  coordinator 134, 140, 142, 150, 158
  earned value 92, 198
  management ix, 7, 25, 26, 30, 135, 185
  milestone 29, 89, 91, 92, 124, 145, 146, 154, 169,
    198
  objectives 16, 19, 38, 85, 96, 127, 140, 198
  partition 21, 24, 64, 84, 110, 127, 134, 156, 166,
    169, 198
  plan ix, 16, 73, 75, 92, 124, 134, 145, 167
  prioritization 27, 49, 54–7, 69, 75, 122, 125, 129
  progress 26, 92, 102, 103, 132, 146
  resources 86
  schedule 90, 198
  scope 6, 19, 49, 63, 75, 78–83, 114, 124, 140
  template 89, 168, 175, 178, 198
Prototype vi, viii, 3, 16, 31, 61, 82, 150, 182, 198
  convergent 62, 82
  design 18, 45, 46, 62, 63, 95, 98, 112–23, 138, 145,
    170, 193
  divergent 62, 82
  look and feel 62, 104, 115, 157, 169, 170
  requirements 5, 8, 61, 62, 198

Q

Quality
  assurance 28, 114, 186
  checking 28, 29, 102, 109, 132, 154
  management 27
  measures 29
  plan 30, 75, 88, 90
  roles 30

R

Rapid application development 3, 198

Relational database vi, 1, 60
Relationship 40, 60
Repeatable process 28
Requirements 12, 17, 57
Resources 6, 25, 86, 199
Responsiveness 16, 54
Reusability x
Reverse engineering 137, 199
Risk 2, 28, 29, 64, 156
    adaptive management 7, 199
    assessment 20, 84, 86
    factors 20, 79
    reduction 174
Roles 17
    fast-track 8–12, 86
    quality 30
    workshop 53

S

Scope creep 54, 129, 140, 158, 199
Scope see Project scope
Scribe 53, 199
Server side see Client/Server
Skills 86
    database 87, 199
    transfer 177
Spaghetti code 137, 199
Spiral life-cycle 3
Sponsor ix, 29, 49, 53, 61, 126, 194, 200
SSADM see Structured Systems Analysis and
        Design Methodology
Stage
    Build 18, 127–64, 167
    Design 95
    Planning 73–94
    Requirements 17, 63, 95–126
    Strategy 16, 17, 185
    Transition 16, 164, 165, 185
Stakeholder 53, 58, 67, 84, 85, 126, 129, 134, 138,
        140, 169, 194, 200
Structured method see Method
Structured Systems Analysis and Design
        Methodology 2
Stub module 70, 71, 98, 116, 118, 146, 200
Style guide vi, 46, 47, 62, 104, 157, 175, 200
Synthesis 182
System 200
    architecture 11, 17, 140, 148, 200
    facility 42, 45, 46, 152, 156, 200
Systems development 1

T

Table 40, 42, 200
Tasks ix, 28
    Build 129–63
    Planning 76–93
    Requirements 99–125
    Transition 166
Team working viii, 30
Techniques ix, 5, 31
    basic 181
    CASE Method 38–49
    evolutionary 8
    fast-track 49–71
Template
    generator 105, 196
    industry 47, 51, 80, 196
    project ix, 89, 168, 175, 178, 198
Test
    acceptance 7, 16, 128, 165
    data for 120, 128, 138, 144, 146, 157, 161
    integration 19, 156–63, 165
    planning of 26, 33–7, 128, 144, 146, 154
    regression 198
    scenario for 34, 128, 156, 158, 160
    unit 154, 201
Third-Generation Programming Language 200
Timebox 6, 21, 25, 90, 146, 158, 160, 200
Timescale 6
Training see User training
Transformer 11, 45, 46, 60, 201
Transition 16

U

Usability 44, 201
User
    acceptance 6, 129, 164
    documentation 128, 149, 151, 161, 165, 170
    help 136, 152, 170
    interface 62
    involvement 7, 24, 127
    need 18
    review 18, 19, 64, 66–70, 118, 135, 138, 154, 159,
        165, 201
    test see Test, acceptance
    training 17, 138, 164, 165
Utility 167, 169, 201

V

Validation rule see Invariant

W

Walkthrough 120, 138, 202
Waterfall life-cycle 2
Work package 90
Workshop 5, 16, 175, 177, 182, 202
   requirements 53, 57–8, 84, 106, 199
   scoping 49–57, 80, 199